IN SEARCH OF THE PERFECT ECONOMIC MATRIX

In Search of the Perfect Economic Matrix

Lawrance George Lux

Writers Club Press

San Jose New York Lincoln Shanghai

In Search of the Perfect Economic Matrix

Writers Club Press
an imprint of iUniverse, Inc.

For information address:
iUniverse, Inc.
5220 S. 16th St., Suite 200
Lincoln, NE 68512
www.iuniverse.com

ISBN: 0-595-25098-X

Printed in the United States of America

Contents

PREFACE

Economists, great and insignificant, focus on some aspect of productive generation, claiming it is the panacea for all economic disturbances. Some say it is government expenditure, some claim financial liquidity, others say it is Government promotion of business. There are the Free Traders, Protectionists, Monetarists, Supply-Siders, Resource Underwriters, Tri-plane Economists, and the Tax Policy Economists (of which the Author is one). This Preface will examine all of the above, before moving on to greater discussion. All share one element in common: No list of economic initiatives works under all economic stress conditions. It can be more simply put: Each proscription runs into it's own set of limitations, causing eventual depressed economic performance and recession.

Free Traders insist economic health resides in the removal to all barriers to Trade, asserting excess production can be disposed Overseas, at profit to the distributing nation. They propose such productive dumping at profit eliminates factors of overproduction, with it's resultant reduction of production, increased unemployment and underemployment, and loss of Profits. They studiously avoid discussion of Transportation Costs; insisting such Costs are only increases of Productive capacity. They refuse commentary on the effect of the spread of technology; simply protesting there are regional advantages of production, without explanation of such advantage loss due to technological refinement. They contend the increasing levels of education for Consumers has no bearing on the analysis, though Market studies assure Consumers quickly drift to the most advanced and efficient product. Their studies do not account for the almost 'Fad' bias inciting major drops in

Sales. Free Trade analysis has only fundamentally fit in study of the 1930s, then only as the alternative which should have been adopted; not in any functioning economic performance.

The Protectionists seem dead in the modern world of Economics, though they really are not. They are simply hidden in another guise. They can be found today in the Conglomeration advocates, who claim capital aggregation provides for real advantages of economic performance. They presently state formalization justifying monopoly conditions, as suitable for modern economic conditions. They advocate relaxation, or elimination, of anti-trust legislation; with concordant theory of major producers buying out minor producers, thereby integrating any and all technological advances made by these smaller companies. Their specialized language calls for price-setting on the part of the Majors, based upon what the Market will bear with studies of Consumption curve ratios; much different from pricing based upon costs of production. They concentrate on Corporate-set schedules of production, rather than Market-generated demand; depending on Marketing strategies to get the appropriate Consumer Demand. Their failure comes from lack of such conquest of Consumer Demand.

Monetarists insist the economic performance of an Economy rests upon the provision of funds for productive energy. The foundation of Monetarist theory comes from study of the industrial societies of the 1930s, a period asserted by all to be an aberration (special case). They quickly point to shortages of the financial supply, to claim cause for any recessive conditions. This purportedly presents justification for their basic hypothesis: Sufficient financial capital can both generate Capitalization for production, and Consumer Demand to provide the profitability for that production. They are somewhat unclear as to what constrains financial flow under normal market conditions, or answer the problem of added costs of production and consumption effect on profitability with the added Credit extension. They cannot provide a real justification for the loss of liquidity from a previous period of high financial reserves. Their analysis of the proposed dis-economies imposed by loss of liquidity lack for verifiable authenticity. They cannot answer the contention the loss of liquidity comes from loss of productive performance: the famous 'Cart before the Horse' issue.

Supply-Sider Economists declare it is the role of Government to promote Business activity. It is overly assertive to say they propose Business welfare, though examination of their tenants brings an effective similarity. None have yet been so blatant, but they would desire elimination of all taxes on Business income. They wish elimination of Capital Gains taxation, insisting Profits on business enterprise should be a Freebie, not taxed as individual income in any way. They would have Government fund all research through a reverse taxation. They insist Government should pay for all needed infrastructure costs, with business enterprise being immune to taxes (property and Sales) organized to pay for such infrastructure costs. They would covet a Government repayment program, which would transfer entrepreneurial risk off the shoulders of Investors, and placing the burden on Consumers through increased taxation. Their program has a rich collection of proposed initiatives, none of which have proven to effectively enhance levels of production, though all promote the individual incomes of business personnel.

Resource Underwriter Economists are little noticed by the Public, though their impact remains huge. Theirs is the policy favored by Landlords. The basic thesis asserts aggregated capital should receive a huge rate of return. Their ideal rate of return would be the ability to pay off any Mortgage within fourteen years, with annual profit to the Mortgage-holder of an additional sixteen percent profit per year. They are adamantly resistant to any reduction of Property values, even to the point of refusal of Sale for years, rather than accept a reduction of price. They insist Property values should increase by Eight percent per year, without consideration of depreciation values. They make little claim to knowledge of methodology in the process of expanding economic performance; except to assert Property values should rise, and property taxes should decrease. They have direct impact upon levels of production, in a very adverse manner; most often seen in the Transport industry, where Prices have continuously risen for half a Century though actual production costs per unit have been going down.

Tri-plane Economists consist of basically reverse Protectionist Economists. They believe all production should be conducted normally, but three Price patterns of Wholesale established for each product, each Price pattern to have it's own marketing strategy. The bottom pattern consists of a Wholesale price for foreign distributors, set to provide a twelve percent profit on production. This price pattern is designed to be competitive in foreign markets against foreign production; expected Sales capable of paying for the cost of Capitalization and maintaining full facility production for extended periods. The second price pattern is designed for a Wholesale price to domestic discount house distributors. The basic price of this pattern allows for an average of about 32% profit on production. This price pattern is not released until some period of time after the last pattern, and designed basically to pay stock dividends to shareholders. The last price pattern is initial Wholesale release to Retail distributors, with a profit ratio of production of around fifty percent. This last pattern is initial release, accompanied with heavy saturation advertising, and designed to acquire 'Fad' consumers. It generally runs for about 8–10 months, before the second pattern release with the advantages of the prior advertising and word-of-mouth spread of product advantage; the foreign release is initiated with the initial release, in conjunction with the heavy advertising saturation.

Tri-plane Economists expect production costs to be paid with foreign Sales, with a price set to be highly competitive. They insist discount house distribution pay stockholder dividends, and suggest lack of such Sales should entail reduction of such dividends; no matter the overall level of profitability for the Company. The initial Retail price release pays for Corporate expansion and the beloved Stock Options of corporate executives; considered absolutely essential by both these executives and Tri-plane Economists. It is easy to perceive domestic

Consumers find themselves paying the highest market prices for products, basically to fuel Corporate expansion and the wealth of the Corporate leadership. The Reverse Protectionism of Tri-plane Economics cost American consumers about thirty percent of their disposable income, as compared to their foreign counterparts; greatest usage laying in Drugs, Medical equipment, Transport equipment, Computer technology, and Fast Food restaurants.

Tax Policy Economists contend Government must assure solid Consumer Demand and restrict Production through proper tax rates. They believe economic performance remains dependent on proper allocation of resources to all Sectors. A fundamental assertion made by them, lies in a tax upon income based solely on largesse; without resort to method derived. This means there would be only an Income Tax—inclusive of Capital Gains, Corporate Tax, and all Excise taxes. Economic performance should be studied by Sector size during periods of economic prosperity, and Excise taxes imposed on Sector production exceeding percentage growth. Liquidity should be maintained by the process of maintaining Governmental surpluses from taxation, which can be lent to the Public through normal deposit in Banks. Tax restrictions should be imposed upon internal financing by Corporations, through tax regulation placing higher taxation based upon undistributed Profits. This factor allows for more uniform growth of personal income by all participants in the business activity, and provides review of capital investment by outside lending institutions. Such a program has never been implemented.

Everyone agrees the Economy must have modified performance factors, eliminating the cyclic performance of Boom and Bust. Most Economists will agree this cyclic performance occurs from dis-equalities of economic development between Sectors. Shortages and Surpluses appear which require reduced production, until the Shortages can be made up, and the surplus stocks reduced. The manner in which elimination of these productive dis-equalities can be achieved, under-scores the entire discussion.

Lawrance George Lux. August 2002.

1

Origins of the Current System

The American economy derives from it's society, as does all else. The earliest drives for American colonial independence came from mercantile interests in the Colonies. These interests faced stiff competition from British companies in the Colonies, and heavy taxation on monopoly purchase prices set by British combines for American merchandise shipped into Great Britain. The above British combines pressured Parliament to forbid Colonial merchants engaging in the Continental markets of Europe, where American colonial merchants could attain prices for their goods from twenty to fifty percent higher. Parliament backed it's order with the British Navy, some historians of this Period of history believe about five percent of all Pirates hung during the Period, were actually American ship masters hauling American goods to Continental ports. Captured American cargos engaged in Continental trade were always sold to the British combines for basically the simple cost to the British Navy, and Prize money to the British seamen. American anger at this practice started to build from about 1530 to 1776, with the loss of about 700 American lives, and a total loss estimated in today's dollars between $30–170 billion; major loss for a basically agrarian society of only cottage industry.

American business interests found further anger in the fact other Colonial powers blocked the internal waterways of the Colonies. Spain held the great drainage basin of the Mississippi, while France (later Britain) held control of the Great Lakes, and Hudson, Ohio, and Tennessee rivers. The western edge of the Colonies could not trade with the build-up East without paying external taxes to foreign powers, because road infrastructure was insufficient for bulk cargo. Western colonial farmers endured only forty percent of the standard of living, which their energies would have granted; except for foreign taxation. Eastern colonial merchants lost approximately thirty percent of their Trade advantage, from exterior Power taxation or restriction. American business interests were ripe for Revolution by 1776.

The American Revolution was basically a Business revolution, and business interests moved to ensure it remains a creature of the business interests. They set specific criteria for election to State and Federal office, mainly based upon property ownership. They maintained control of all Revolutionary Committees, which dispossessed Royalists according to the desires of business interests; who soon acquired these properties at advantageous prices. The Continental Congress had to purchase all supplies for Itself and the Army from Colonial suppliers; a practice granting business interests a minimum of middleman profits. Business found Revolution to be extremely profitable, especially as they could block effective taxation.

It is interesting to note about 47% of American property changed hands through this process, and funds of purchase were designated to pay for the expense of the Continental Army and the Revolutionary Congress. Both entities ran at a deficit throughout the Revolution. The cost of the Continental Army never actually exceeded any State budget of the Period; heavily engaged in payment of militia forces to fulfill orders for Revolutionary committees. Some real good bargains came from Revolutionary Committee sale of Royalist property. One of the fundamental factors leading to the Constitutional Convention was the huge debt of the national government under the Articles of Confederation; the Convention called to determine ways to pay off this debt.

Business accounting procedures continued in force throughout this Period, and clear to the present day. The last of the Continental Army soldiers were paid off with land grants on the Western frontier in 1791.

Failures of Federal wage payments to it's workers persisted until the mid-1830s. No Congress since 1776 has failed to raise taxes or debt issuance to pay for business claims of supply to the Government, whether these claims had validity or not. These same Congresses have funded 93% of all Government projects favored by the business interests of the nation or region, in which such projects were to be completed; this compares with about fifty percent for projects of popular demand, but without the support of business interests.

A study conducted at the State level, the case of Erie Canal and New York, indicates almost seventy percent of the New York populace initially opposed this construction. Supposition studies (based on hypotheses of operational effect) estimate New York taxpayers paid approximately eight percent of their yearly income throughout the construction of the Erie Canal, and three percent of their income for maintenance of the Canal throughout it's operating history. Business interests paid for about twenty percent of the initial capitalization, and nothing for it's maintenance.

Construction of the Erie Canal cost New York taxpayers about as much as the Interstate system today costs the American taxpayer. The business interests of New York increased their volume of business about 17 times with the opening of the Erie Canal, with a profit of about Eight percent on total volume. American business interests today produce about sixty percent of the volume of traffic on the Interstate system, causing almost 83% of the deterioration of the road system; while paying about thirteen percent of the total cost of construction and maintenance of the Interstate system. The interplay of business interests in American politics still exists.

The above information supplies background to the first axiom of American Politics: American business interests will always force American taxpayers to pay for desired business developments, which they themselves do not wish to underwrite because of lack of profit or degree of risk. They accomplish this goal through political contributions, and by control of the local and State Party machinery. They pass judgement on all political candidates, refusing Party endorsement on any who will not submit to business interests demands; then control almost seventy percent of the political campaign contributions, garnering ability to insist on specific issues. Examination of the results of American business political actions highlights better than any discussion.

The first great American wave development was the creation of the railway system. Business interests enjoined Congress to provide land grants for rail line development, some three times the area actually necessary; purpose: sale of such lands was to pay for the system development. Actual construction was financed by Communities raising funds to be included in the system, and private subscriptions and bonds. The touted reason behind all railroad drives was faster and cheaper transportation. A Public Relations campaign brought huge subscription funds. The rest of the story tells the tale.

The Railroads sold the land grants for approximately 27 times the cost of construction and maintenance of the lines. Bondholders and Communities received about twenty-five cents on the dollar for their subscription, then only after long delays of payment; in violation of bond issuance rates. Many communities promised access to the proposed lines found themselves off the lines after subscription payments; the purported reason being geographic considerations forestalling construction. Railroads undercut wagon freighters all along the line until the freighters went into bankruptcy, then raised cargo rates one-quarter on average over the previous wagon freight rates. Passenger rates were always higher, because of the speed and ease of transport. The Age of wealthy Railroad magnates was born.

The Second Great wave was the ironclad, steam-driven shipping lines. Shipyards received their government welfare by production of American naval vessels. Some economic studies indicate final delivery cost to the Government vastly exceeded construction costs to the shipyards; a factor aided by Congressional laws prohibiting foreign construction of US naval vessels. Congress often awarded said Contracts for naval vessels to Shipyards lacking the capital capacity to build such vessels, fronting the funds to Shipyards to build the necessary capacity. This allowed these Shipyards to enter cargo vessel construction with provided Government capitalization, after they had completed the prerequisite naval vessels. The Author believes the Shipyards were paid almost Nine times the actual production cost of the naval vessels, by the final payment at delivery. Future contracts for naval vessels did not diminish in cost, though the necessary capitalization was already present.

The shipping lines received their Government favoritism by Congressional action limiting certain types of cargo, and all Government shipping, to American shipping lines. American shipping lines could afford to set some of the highest shipping rates in the World, after 1885. It is interesting to note all maintained two-tier shipping freight rates, dependent on the national origin of the consignor; domestic paying much more. It became cheaper to ship a ton of material from China to San Francisco, than an equal amount from Charleston to New York. The Age of the Shipping Magnates was born.

The third Great wave, concurrent with the first two, was Industrialization. Business induced Congress to relax immigration rules, and allow importation of unskilled labor without restraint. Business pressured for Protectionist tariffs and obtained them until the end of the 1920s. Business forced American consumers to pay higher prices for an incredible range of consumer products, than was present elsewhere in the World. We have led the World in Consumer pricing for over a Century. Nine countries in the World have higher per capita income than does the United States, but American consumer product pricing matching any country in the World.

The Fourth Great wave was Road Transport, but the Interstate system has already been discussed. Sufficient for the discussion is the statement Americans pay as high a construction price for roadway and street, as is possible to be found in the World. Condemnation of private property for roadways continues at a frantic pace, with loss to the tax base. Every tax in place to pay for such construction, business either has immunity from the tax, or gains a tax rebate from the Federal government for such expense.

The Fifth Great wave has been the development of Utilities. Business rants and raves today about Government setting of Consumption rates. They fail to mention Government has guaranteed profitability to these industries since their inception, with Government transfer payments made to utilities whenever such profitability failed. They do not comment on the free access granted for utilities passage and lines across Government property. The nuclear industry fails to clarify their immunity from lawsuit and damages from accidents. They leave unsaid statements codifying Government-regulated freight rates on their sources of fuel. They omit conversation discussing Federally-guaranteed loans, and freedom from private audit of expenses by the Public.

Telecommunications is currently in trouble as of this writing. The overwhelming component of this trouble shows as overpayment of dividends and Executive salaries and Stock Options through the previous years. Consumer consumption of provided services has been increasing at a arithmetic rate, since the dawn of the industry. Price rates for such Consumption has also been increasing at a steady rate. Overcapitalization of Telecommunication occurs only from mistakes of Management in the industry; mistakes driven by an assessed forty percent profit on all construction—vastly increasing capitalization costs while reducing actual equity. Business would claim the trouble lie in the fault of Government regulation; while Business has been in charge of the stated regulation, since the Reagan administration.

American business possess an advantageous position in the World market, through reduced employee training costs. They actually pay only about half of the training costs of their foreign counterparts. They utilized the property tax-funded educational system traditionally; and when this system failed to provide labor of sufficient specialization, they induced the Government to fund the Community college system. They can send employees to such institutions for specialized instruction, paying only for tuition—subsidized with two-thirds of the cost being borne by taxpayers. They set up the social milieu whereby it is expected of parents and Government grants to pay for higher education, and reimburse with only about eighty percent of the salaries paid by foreign competitors (this estimated as a percentage share of area standards of living). They are cheap, even when it comes to paying the help.

American business, especially since the Bush Tax Cut, enjoy the best tax position of Anyone in the World. Some eighty Corporations received tax rebates on taxes which they did not pay in the first place, under the Bush Tax Cut. They should have paid those taxes, but did not, because of existing tax deferments, credits, and exemptions; which did not stop the tax rebates. They seek to eliminate Capital Gains taxation and Inheritance taxation; again trying to shift the tax burden to labor and Consumer.

Thirty percent of American production is conducted on Trade-free zones, providing immunity from local taxation. This compares quite well with foreign competition, who generally average about a 17% payment of Profits as local taxation. American business also saves about thirty percent of the costs of transportation, through taxpayer underwriting of said costs of road tax; and Government subsidy of business transportation expense. It is no wonder American business can afford a rate of capitalization almost three times that of most Competitors, while paying the highest Corporate salaries in the World. Stock dividends for American corporations, regrettably, remain almost uniform with other stocks in the World.

Great mention has been made of Stock Options lately, those made by the Author not the least. It is true Stock Options are utilized by almost all Corporations today. They were introduced as a method to replace payment of increased Executive salaries. Certain facts about Stock Options should be known by stockholders and the Public. The first fact consists of the degree of use by American corporations, who have used Stock Options in total dollar value terms; almost 37 times as often as any other foreign corporations. American Corporations limit such use of Stock Options to only twenty percent of the employees, as is traditional in foreign corporations. Foreign Corporations issue such Stock Options per employee, about three times in average per forty year career. American Corporations make such Stock Options available on a yearly basis to the select few of employees granted such options; some Executives are granted these Stock Options up to Eight times a year. American use of Stock Options does differ from International use, and carries great risk of Stock value and dividend loss over the long run.

Most Readers would supposition the Author has distinct bias against the Business interests. Any bias derives from the economic losses brought on by such favoritism of Business interests, as shown by American Government. A colleague remarks the Author expresses no sympathy for American labor, who is heavily invested in the Stock Market for pension and retirement funds. The Author, in reality, attempts to triple the return dividends made to stockholders of all levels. Readers will begin to doubt at this point; such claims of immediate wealth often made by hawkers for the Stock Market. Read the next Chapter!

2

The current economic milieu consists of the product of American legislative act, at all levels of government. Local governments differentiate between residential and commercial property, allowing and encouraging a two-tier expense assessment system. Commercial property sits on approximately 35% of the property tax base, but pays less than ten percent of the property taxes. They do this through outright dismissal of such taxes, or commercial rates of payments near half of residential property tax rates.

Traffic patterns indicate eighty percent of all Workweek travel migrates to and from these commercial sites. Traffic patterns to these sites demand special main route construction, due to the numbers involved. This construction must be paid by property taxation or use-taxes such as a fuel tax. Business pays only about ten percent of the property tax today, and the fuel tax is deductible as expense to business; or shifted to workers and transport independents for payment. Their payment share of infrastructure costs while producing almost three-quarters of the traffic, stands at approximately eight percent of total cost.

Alternate Government action gains further advantages for the business interests, for which taxpayers must pay. All utilities grant reduced rates for volume usage of their service or product. The volume of usage by business literally quadruples the operating costs of these utilities, but reduced rates for volume allowed business to pay only about forty percent of the operating cost. Minimal service users (residential households) must pay almost seven times what their usage actually costs to provide.

A cell-phone costing Nine cents a minute to Individual subscriber, so multi-access customers can pay 1.5 cents a minute. Seven cents out of Nine paid by Individual subscribers, actually pays for the capacity of telecommunication companies to provide for the needs of the multi-access users. This provision has to be made, but must Individual subscribers pay for it? This example was chosen because it reflects no expectation of discrimination by the Public, and less discriminatory cost to Individual users in dollar terms; than do other Utilities like Power, Water, or Garbage collections.

The average rate of pay for American workers is highly debatable today, all because of the matrix of occupations which should be included. This average rate of pay estimates run from $8.35 per hour, to about $16.04 cents an hour. This variance mainly comes from Accounting procedures, which may or may not include retirement and medical benefits, the Issue of whether these benefits are paid or only promised without payment, and determinations of what is management versus labor positions. The entire discussion is immaterial to the Issue at hand, except to give a range of labor costs for business. Full payment of local tax burden plus full utility expense paying for total usage, would produce an additional hourly wage cost of between an estimated $.85 per hour to $3.04 per hour. Understand these are averages, and do not reflect the hourly costs of energy-intensive industrial processes.

Little information can be picked from any economic reports about the next average considered. Supposition studies (based on realistic expectation guesses) indicate business profit per worker hour ranges from $12.25 to $31, for a national average. The national average cost of capitalization (repayment plus interest) has an estimate range of between $6 and $8 per hour. Business profit per labor hour after payment of expenses have an estimated range of between $6.25 and $23 per national hour of labor. A Two dollar per labor hour profit has been estimated capable of all recapitalization expense with a Two percent rate of growth. The Author projects Business could pay it's full share of the local property tax burden, as well as full utilities' expenses from operation; all without detriment to operational viability.

State and Federal tax regulation gives business interests equally privileged position. States do not charge Business any sales tax upon Wholesale purchases or sales. They do not charge for the purchase of resources, and give rebates of sales tax to business interests in their purchase of operating equipment. This saves Business an operating expense which could not exceed eight percent of their operating costs. Most Reader would think this beneficial for Business. A more detailed examination could shed further light.

Failure to fully tax all Sales, including Wholesale and resources, costs almost a tripling of the Sales tax rates among the several States and local communities. This is a direct percentage decrease of Consumer spending, taxes acquired instead of Consumer Goods. The national average would be about a Five percent reduction in Consumption. A tax on all Sales would reduce this loss to less than Two percent. What would be the impact of imposition of full tax on all Sales?

Retail and Discount houses average a 44% markup over Wholesale costs on a national average. This averages a national Profit over retailing and marketing expenses of about an estimated 12–26 percent profit over the range of Wholesale costs of product purchase. Current Sales tax rate could not absorb even eight percent of such Profits, and adequately adjusted Sales tax rates would bring a loss of no more than Two percent of this Profit. An estimated Three percent increase in Consumer Consumption could actually increase actual dollar profits.

Examination of the Corporate Income tax structure imposed by the Federal Government shows vast hazard to economic performance. Their separation from Personal Income tax alone is a preferential treatment, allowing for special tax dispensations not open to the individual taxpayer. They receive a tax rate lower than some Individual taxpayers, though their average taxable income stands at a level almost 340 times the average income level of personal individuals. Various Tax studies have been undertaken throughout the years, but most who have studied the Issue; impress that each Corporate dollar excused from taxation, mean approximately three dollars more which personal income tax payers must pay. Other economic studies indicate better than half of all tax dollars released to personal income taxpayers, will translate into added Consumer Consumption. What can an Economist determine from this data?

The competent Economist would say it expresses need for more information, for translatable economic projection. The Author was privy to a private, unpublished study which indicated every dollar borrowed by Government (Federal, State, or Local), did cause $.0274 of inflation in prices in the Resource market. The study remains silent through fear of the Corporate management employing the economists involved in the Study.

This evidence denies the Keynesian hypothesis under normal conditions, because the resultant inflationary pressure subtracts economic momentum from the government spending. It does not nullify Keynesian thought, during times of deep retraction of Resource consumption. Other economic studies express tendencies of Resource consumption reduction occur only with an unemployment rate greater than Nine percent as a national average. This means Keynesian deficit spending by Governments should only be used after such unemployment rates are sustained, for a period of longer than three months.

Current economic initiatives by the Bush administration place sharp inflationary pressure on the Resource market prices, which can be found to be rising. This pressure is not reflected in Consumer retail prices, because of Business fears of Consumption reductions. It is directly reflected in the current round of Layoffs and downsizing. The Bush administration is also hiding the amount of debt they are accumulating, to defuse possible discredit to the Bush Tax Plan. The Author estimates this aggregation of increased debt load will produce a Seven percent increase in Resource prices, by the middle of 2003. The increase in prices in the Resource market will wipe out of advantages to Business from the tax reductions of the Bush Plan, by the beginning of 2004.

Supply-Side Economists have always insisted tax breaks for Business would provide fuel to spur the economy. Their general hypothesis states anything which reduces the operating costs of Business will lead to greater aggregations of capital for investment purposes. They pointedly ignore several relevant factors. The first and greatest remains unnamed; their entire reference point revolves around building the ability of Business to internally finance capital growth.

There are several economic detriments to internal financing. Internal financing does not utilize the same criteria as do lending institutions. Most do not utilize production, packaging, transport, marketing, retailing, and warehouse cost breakdowns; as any financial institution would insist upon in a Prospectus. A lending institution insists on a seventy percent probability of schematic profitability to approve a loan. No Corporate internal financing design has ever used this strict observance to the knowledge of the Author.

Current Federal Tax regulations require capital investment in order to exercise the tax credits available to business. This means Business must invest, or pay their assessed tax load. The pressure is on the Corporate structure to invest, whether there is a viable investment opportunity or not. Internally financed Corporate investment has traditionally been based on studies establishing parameters of the greatest amount which could be lost, many deliberately entered into knowing these investments would operate at a loss. Neither proper care or good judgement enters into Corporate internal financing, such investment orchestrated by individuals not trained in investment finance; but rather in structuring management goal fulfillment.

The use of internal financing by Corporations also basically eliminates any exterior supervision of Corporate activity. The Board of Directors whose mission is to supervise Corporate operations, are too often picked by Management. Their introduction to the same reward packages which Management grants to itself, cuts any sharp critique of Management policy. Stockholders find themselves with no advocate at Court.

The extension of Management rewards insures the Corporate operations are conducted for the benefit of Management. Stockholders, Employees, and Consumers suffer from the mismanagement; Stockholders through loss of undistributed Profits which feed the Management rewards system, Employees from reduced wages and overwork from downsizing to feed the reward system of Management, and Consumers through inferior products and higher prices.

Government regulation of business activity lacks complete viability, through a number of factors. Such regulation which is not based upon a tax system will never work. The gain from malfeasance will always exceed the fines imposed, which are always long-delayed through a arbitration system which can only benefit the Violator by delays and reduced fines upon appeal. Good legal representation can gain such advantage, funds even held in simple bank notes; can possibly double the assessed fine before it is paid. The Violator is allowed to keep and use all funds during the period of arbitration. There are Companies still contesting fines for violations committed in the 1950s. The Bush administration allowed a power plant to be reopened, which had been closed a half-dozen years before, after being ordered shut down during the Nixon administration. It will probably take longer to shut it down this time.

Government regulation depends upon Government supervisory personnel to provide inspection. Congressional appropriations provide funding for full-time supervision of a total of three percent of all economic activity in this Country. A power plant may receive one inspection every three years, with operations set up to switch to cheaper violation practices within simple hours of maintenance. Only Four percent of Surprise Inspections by supervisory personnel are actually a surprise to the business operations concerned, who manage to get an average four days notice of the inspections. The noncompliance with operating regulations often makes these concerns up to $100,000 per day, while the maximum of fines imposed rarely exceed $10,000 per day. There is always a Court available to Business, for the reversal of any adverse regulatory agency decision.

Republican Congresses of the 1990s felt the pain of poor individual taxpayers over the rude, inconsiderate behavior of the Internal Revenue Service. They decided to castrate the IRA to save individual taxpayers such pain. A side effect of this castration was placement of the burden of proof upon the IRS, who had to submit to the restrictions of law enforcement established for the prosecution of criminal proceedings. A beneficial effect for business interests (an assured by-product, never intended) was the IRS's need to prove business interests were withholding financial records; the IRS mandated to provide evidence of criminal intent, prior to being issued subpoena or search warrant. Business interests found their financial records safe from prying Eyes, and could conduct their affairs in a manner profitable to themselves; without enduring the horrid expense of taxation.

American business, today, suffers terribly from Governmental constriction. Only 82% of the regulatory agents and enforcers, who oversee compliance with Federal regulations, have previously worked in the industry; and maintained their associations with people still working in the industry. Regulators only spend 70% of their consultation time and 83% of the hearings testimony with the leadership of the regulated industry; the rest of the time is spent with Environmental protection or Consumer protection advocates. Only 55% percent of the Federal regulators learn their jobs well enough to later accept positions with the industry regulated.

Courts rule in favor of industry lawyers only 62% of the time, when contested by Government regulators, Consumer advocates, or Environmental advocates. No industry has yet paid over forty percent of the cleanup costs engendered by an adverse Court decision on some biohazard issue. There is some rational speculation American taxpayers spend approximately $211in eventual taxation, for every dollar American business interests spend on legal fees. They seek to free themselves from this expense, by legislation forestalling lawsuit claims being filed against them, and limitation of awards if the lawsuits cannot be stopped. This effort finds aid through legislative action continually reducing the time allowed under Statute of Limitations provisions.

Open any national business trade magazine and One can read of the horrible victimization American business suffers at the hands of Government. American business supplies at least three-quarters of the political campaign contributions of the nation, through the Owners, Employees, or tax-deductible PAC soft money grants; this not counting the check-box contributions on Income Tax returns. American business interests must feel bruised by the indifference expressed by Politicians towards them. Their access to these Politicians remains at a measly 90%, while the check-box contributors get a whole ten percent of political access. The worst discrimination comes from legislative bills introduced into the Congressional hopper for consideration as law, a whole thirty percent of those initiatives are not business-sponsored. American business must feel so bad, as they threaten to move off-shore at one Republican colleague suggests; ruthlessly abandoning Sales in the American market. We must save American business from the totalitarian system of the American democratic process!

3

Investment

A probable half of all economic model studies devote concentration to maximization of investment. Investment is the great God of Economics; economic growth a purported function of investment. A rare few detractor studies ask disquieting questions about what effect investment could have upon the rate of inflation. Suggested facts have derived from these studies: a rate of investment less than 7.4% for a greater period than three years, will lead to a drop of economic performance due to over-aging capital equipment (downtime and maintenance costs); almost one percent of all investment must be devoted to stockpiling resource materials, or result in serious drops in production time profitability; the investment rate must be higher than 8% of total volume of Sales (in dollars term), in order to generate increases of production (after a three-shift, 48 hour Workweek has been adopted); investment of over 11% of total volume of Sales will lead to inflationary pressure on the Resource and capital equipment supply markets; and Sales must remain steady or increase, if production time productivity ratios are not lost from capital equipment.

The ratio of 7.4% indicates the level of recapitalization necessary under continuing Sales. Recapitalization rates can be maintained at less than 7.4%, because of declining Sales and reduced labor force, but a drop in capital equipment will be realized. The ratio of 7.4% will not maintain recapitalization under stable or increasing Sales, because some of the ratio has been eaten up by resource material stockpiling. Under increasing Sales, or prolonged periods of stable Sales, the investment ratio must equate to around 8.4%; in order for adequate recapitalization schedules to be maintained. The variance between products in the above ratios can be as high as 1.7%, while the ratios variance between industries can be almost three percent due to the nature of the capital equipment.

The decision for capital equipment expansion vary due to constrictions of Plant size, transport through the Plant area, and the cost of resource materials. Applications of the above factors will reduce capital equipment expansion to a potential zero. Another limiting factor is the ability to expand from a two-shift to a three-shift production day; this shift costing almost a four percent increase in unit product costs, due to increased welfare payments and wage differentials for the second and late shifts. A single-shift production day indicates not only a cost-ineffective loss of capital equipment, but functional limitation to capital growth; until there is shift to a full three-shift operating day. Recapitalization costs for a one-shift production day are almost seventy percent of the same costs for a three-shift production day; reflecting the inflexibility of such costs, and functionally doubling the capital equipment cost per unit of production.

Labor training costs will always absorb approximately twenty percent of the total capital expansion expenditure for the first year. Production ratios will not peak until the third year of capital expansion. The production ratio, averaged, will be around seventy-five percent of an experienced line, over the three-year period. Leveraged Capital expansion thereby assumes the three-year cost of loan interest, plus productivity declines of one-quarter of whatever percentage such new equipment equates for production. This will translate to a 6% higher production cost for all produced product off the new equipment, plus a surcharge for interest of 1–2% (the rates will vary according to the Model formulation, but equivalences basically remain). This translates directly as a loss of Profits of 8%, throughout the total produced units of the new capital equipment.

The above analysis gives the basic cost of capital equipment expansion, which has a variance between products of almost four percent, and between industries of less than three percent. The element of Overtime must be considered in the equation. A defined labor production operation will find little value in Overtime past 56 hours, because of full manning of capital equipment. Most wage rates are set, so that such levels of Overtime will not expand production unit costs above twelve percent. Product scarcity will raise product price, so further capital expansion can generally be deemed unnecessary; unless Consumer demand for the product has risen over fourteen percent, a position determined to pay for the above extended production of initial capital expansion. The resort to the extensive Overtime is of limited duration, with labor refusal to continue the regime without huge wage increases. Productivity reductions can be expected as well; Overtime labor will only be 87% as productive as ordinary labor, and losses of 2% of productivity per week will accrue from extended periods of full Overtime, after an initial five weeks.

[Layman Translation: The above simply implies production expansion will incur loss of product unit profitability, unless Consumer Demand stands higher than 114% of full production from a three-shift—40 Workweek facilities in a seasonal pattern for over 14 weeks (two 5-week period of 56 hours of Overtime, separated by a 4-week period of Labor rest at 40 hours with sale of Inventory. This seasonal pattern can also be met with two 8-week periods of 48 hours a week, separated by a 4-week period, if there is excess Inventory storage space. This presupposes year-round Consumer Demand of 100%, and a 3-shift Work force. This entails only a 12% loss of product unit profitability from Overtime, with a 13% loss of productivity levels during Overtime hours, as compared with Capital Expansion costs which likely will incur a 43% profitability unit loss, and 25% loss of productivity levels over three years.]

Many businesses hope to pay for new capital expansion through movement into new marketing areas. The marketing efforts in the new marketing areas will cost an additional fifteen percent of product unit loss for three years, and Sales volume probably not equal to volumes from established marketing areas in that period. The entire effort will likely cost an additional ten+ percent increase in unit production costs(including marketing) for the entire Product line over the three years. Capital equipment expansion and marketing costs are such most businesses will find it impractical, unless an sustained increase in Sales between 23–25% can be maintained after three years. Capital expansions should be of such magnitude as production can be conducted with at most a three-shift Forty hour Workweek for workers for the quarter expansion..

Entrance into new marketing areas suffer immensely from competition of equivalent technology products. The presence of four equivalent products meeting the introductory product will assure only a twenty percent share of the market after three years, if two of these products enjoy the same marketing resources as does the introductory product. Sustained increase in Sales of between 23–25% increase after three years will require entrance into numerous marketing areas, if their volume is not sufficiently large; at doubling or more of marketing budgets for the introductory product, and continued advertising cost increases against competitive products in the market..

Most Corporate managements of multi-product companies hold the erroneous belief marketing can be expanded to encompass a new product, with only a arithmetic increase in marketing budgets. This is simply not true! The Consumer market must be targeted, both in magnitude and Sales rate. The specific marketing program to attract these Consumers must be chosen; also a specific Ad line formation, else over half the market will not be attracted. Use of an older Ad-line formation will have only possess eighty percent effectiveness, due to drift inoculation of Consumers from repeated message, and failure to cross all marketing areas with the new Ad-line will incite loss of five percent of Sales in already established marketing areas. This raises the advertising costs to a full Ad line distribution. A specific advertising medium matrix must be chosen, to bring the campaign within the specific marketing cost per unit; a element needed to be picked during the initial production expansion decision. A refusal to implement the full program will fall short of marketing goals, or will vastly exceed any realistic marketing cost per unit through excessive marketing ad replacement.

[Layman translation: Product production expansion should be expanded in minimums of 25% of full capacity per expansion, to avoid dis-economies of scale(too expensive financial charges, overcharging by Millwright labor, training cost overruns, and unnecessary losses of production schedules. Market conditions of competitive product insist marketing effort into a wider market must actually be 2.5 times the Consumer Demand arena, as the current established market for present production contains. Market saturation of old and new markets of such size will demand a marketing budget 3.7 times the previous marketing budget for saturation over three years, and 2.5 times current marketing budget after three years, for full production Sales. This does not include the 12% product unit loss for eight months of the three year Period, due to Overtime needs in the established production line; to correct shortfalls of production from the new line. The old production level returns to full unit profitability only after 1.4 years, considering the increased marketing cost, while the new lines reaches same unit profitability only after approx. fifty months.

Superior technology product introduction against competition entails the same level of marketing effort, with indications market goals will not be reached with product price levels greater than 2% greater than the Consumer utility increase in percentage (CU+2%). This analysis is fairly standard, whether the production is internally-expanded or by Buyout. Variance between product and industry, though, can be as high as eighty percent, but extreme losses of product unit profitability must always be expected for extended periods]

External financing through lending institutions demands submission of a Prospectus. Efficient management of lending institutions will insist all the above calculations be included in the Prospectus, plus numerous other evaluations. The lending institutions will want to know the size of the potential market, how great a percentage of market share can be gained per increment of marketing budget, the variance of Consumer demand per percentage alteration in product price, the stability of resource materials pricing, the potential market share loss incurred by competitive product reductions in price, the time required for full marketing saturation, the matrix of marketing medium through which market saturation will take place, whether production can match Sales rates under market marketing saturation—falling short of demand or creating a surplus of product, the recovery rate of selling at discount rates, the packaging costs, and the transportation costs. They will want a definitive unit cost per product through sale of that product, and a defined estimate of the unit profit to be made; all within the matrix of a realizable Sales projection.

Lending institutions will make their determination on financing the capital expansion based upon a seventy percent probability of Prospectus goals being met, if down-the-road refinancing debt service can recover any projected losses. Considerations used in this analysis consist of the estimated saturation of the market without introductory product, realistic production and marketing analysis of Prospectus indicating discount pricing of product could recover the loan plus interest, estimated stability in production and marketing costs, and the total net equity of the Company minus the debt level. Such institutions will turn down any Prospectus which they estimate debt service could not be maintained, at a level of Two percent profit per unit for the Corporation; this to insure protection from flux in resource material pricing, or introduction of technologically superior competition marketing.

Corporate internal financing functions along quite dissimilar lines. The Author knows of no Corporate board which uses even thirty percent of the analysis expressed above. Corporate boards consist of memberships not conversant with analysis studies. Major Corporations (GM, IBM, United Technologies, and Microsoft etc.) often approve a product addition, based solely on mention the company should enter the area. A voice vote is taken and approved, without any Cost or Price analysis at all. Every employee of the Corporation then fulfills the parameters of their own expertise, and the Board reviews only the first Sales report on the approved product. The Author has personally witnessed the production of products in this manner, where the total cost per product unit exceeded the average sale price of competitive products in a very competitive market by a multiple of three; necessitating a 'Rolls Royce' superiority marketing strategy, which rarely even covers the marketing costs.

Approximately twenty percent of the approved product lines of internal Corporate financing cannot bring product unit cost after Sale below the average sale price of competitive products. An additional sixty percent of approved product lines of internal Corporate financing, must sell those products at less than four percent profit per unit, in order to get enough Sales to continue the production line. Less than Six percent of approved product lines of internal Corporate financing operate at standard profit per unit ratios of the successful products in the market.

Corporate internal finance does far better with the process of buying new product lines, through the purchase of smaller companies in Buyouts. The process, though, has many economic detriments. The overwhelming destruction comes in the form of excessive purchase price—an average with often requires almost 23 years of production to pay for the dollar amount of purchase, if standard production and marketing costs are utilized. This is far too high, as full production facilities still have to be capitalized, and marketing share derived.

The second great destruction comes in the method of payment for such acquisitions: eight-five percent of the purchase price is paid in stock of the purchasing company. Dilution of parent company stock is entailed, with a loss in stock dividends to all stockholders equal to about 1.7 times the purported value of the purchase. Eight to Ten acquisitions of this order can reduce the equity of stockholders in the parent company to less than ten percent of their original equity, and reduce their dividends by three-quarters through spread numbers of shares. Acquisition of four to six product lines by Buyout, which shows only mediocre performance; often eliminates any dividends at all, with the product line dis-economies and stock dilution destroying profits' viability in successfully profitable product lines previously held.

One of the worst factors of Corporate buyouts to increase product lines comes from overcapacity of production facilities. Candidates for Buyout have inevitably established a position in a specialized market. Their production facilities already effectively feed an innate market very successfully. Often further Sales could only be accomplished with advertising-created markets. Innate markets will maintain a replacement level of Sales, over the period of product durability. Created markets induce compulsive 'Fad' purchasing, which has no replacement market. Individuals will not repurchase, or they will purchase alternative products to study differences of characteristics. Fad purchasers are simply one-time purchasers, with no product loyalty; the original innate market already supplied with sufficient product; the resulting production destined for discount houses at Wholesale prices barely above production costs.

Corporate Parents always insist on expansion of product line production facilities, hoping to capture the Fad market. Capitalization averages quadrupling the original production facilities. A major marketing campaign introduced to excite the Fad market, bringing all advertising and production costs associated with new line production. Initial Sales are often high, but drop off after the first year of full production operation; with marketing dollars, no matter how extreme, producing only about 18–20% of the previous year's Sales. Full production facilities function at only a fifth of productive capacity, Parent companies run such operations at a four to seven percent loss, and stockholders lose dividends because of a operational volume of about seventeen percent of the purchase price per year.

Tax policy Economists (the Author plus others) possess an abhorrence of internal Corporate financing policies. They feel so strongly, they advocate a stiff, graduated Excise Tax upon all undistributed Corporate profits. This Excise tax should equal an estimated Twelve percent of the amounts, plus the average bank interest charges on lending such an amount. This tax should increase by Five percent, with every additional increment of ten million dollars of undistributed Corporate profits. Normal recapitalization of existing capital would not be taxed, being considered as normal expense of operations. This would be combined with complete elimination of all Corporate tax credits for investment; they left with the normal expense of debt service from lending institutions as deductible expense from Taxes.

The dividend rates of Principal/Dividend would reduce substantially, producing more rapid doubling of investment. Capital gains would produce much higher tax revenues, with early un-delayed dividend payments; as well as Corporate Income tax receipts. Such reserves would pass through lending institutions at accelerated rates, producing more rapid aggregation of capital for investment; than is found in the current Corporate structure of fund retention. Corporations would be forced to seek external financing for capital growth investments, forcing them to abide with proper rules of investment procedure. The increased rate of loan application would provide a better rate of return for bank depositors, while the value of Stocks would accrue in value, because of the higher rates of return.

The previous policy stands as anathema to standard Economic policy. Supply-Side Economists would assert such a policy robs Corporations of economic initiative, adequate supply of operating funds, and requires payment of too excessive a tax rate for economic growth. The paperwork and delays associated with external financing would retard economic growth, and limit such growth to acceptable level of risk growth ratios; undercutting rapid economic expansion. They assert the level of economic performance and it's growth is fundamental to maintenance of Consumer Demand through payment of salaries. They claim Unemployment rates would rise because of reduced economic activity, and interest rates would drop through underutilization of financial funds. They would finish with a statement that the reduced rate creation of a wealthy class would reduce the provision of risk capital.

Monetarist Economists would argue such profits distribution would reduce the Money Supply, because of the increased rate of Consumption by recipients; who would purportedly reduce their savings ratio, if allowed personal decision. The increased rate of Consumption would raise resource prices, and constrict Corporate operating funds needed with the added Consumption, due to the dictated external financing. Bank debt service charges would increase as interest rates to depositors would need increase, to combat the increased attractiveness of stock through the increased dividends. They would insist the flow of the Money Supply would be curtailed, due to the enforced external financing with service charges; and bank reserves would have to be reduced, to maintain the proper flow of funds. Corporate growth rates would be restricted by external financing with increased debt charges; inciting a higher rate of unemployment.

Tri-plane Economists rebel completely, knowing capital investment funds would not shift beyond the area of lending institution operation. Such funds would go to stockholders, to be deposited in lending institutions of their home areas. Foreign capitalization would have to be accomplished by loans between lending institutions, and subject to the lending restrictions of the lender. Profits from Corporate operations would return to stockholder origin, forestalling Corporate evasion of taxation. The flow of capital would reverse, with profits returning to the home of the lending institutions. The increased income of Consumers in the home market would shift production to domestic consumption, entailing higher foreign market prices because of shortage of supply. Competitive advantage would be lost in foreign markets, increasing the price of foreign raw materials, and increasing the wage levels of foreign labor; now utilized for profit-taking.

Free Traders join with the Tri-plane Economists, knowing such tax regulation would slow Corporate expansion to an International level. The exterior financing restrictions placed upon Corporations limit competition in international markets at prices below the profitability associated with externally-financed production (a complex manner to explain product dumping could no longer be exercised for foreign product demand). Transportation costs would again assert their positional power, as Corporations could not discount them; being externally financed. Resource pricing would suffer downward price pressure, as other Corporate costs would rise in relation to them, reducing consumption below current market curves. Mass marketing internationally of standard products in the face of competition would become much more expensive, as Corporate internally-financed cost-skating could not be conducted. The volume of World Trade could be expected to reduce by 15–30%, and revert to specialized, technological products and base resources.

Resource Underwriter Economists take umbrage at such tax policy, as it raises the value of both stock and band deposits in relation to Property. Commercial Property will lose current rates of profitability, as lending institutions insist usage must reduce in cost; all to provide for loan viability. Residential property will lose in value, as investment elsewhere becomes more attractive; because of the excessive pricing of existing property. The Author asserts an Individual can purchase a building design, hire construction workers, pay them the highest trade rates, build a Two million dollar residence; at a price considerably less than a half million, possibly excluding the land on which it is built. A percent increase in the standard rates of return on investments would likely decrease demand for residential property by a likely Four percent, equating to a eventual residential price reduction of 8–9% over-all.

Protectionist Economists would not approve of the tax policy either, losing the protective tax credits for business enterprise. Business would have to face unrestricted competition, would not be able to build capital reserves for Corporate takeovers, and could not maintain monopoly or oligarchical prices. Unprofitable ventures would be divested by order of lending institutions, who would limit credit upon refusal. They would lose the omnipotent mega-Corporation which they love so much; forced out of oligarchical forms of market control. Market pricing would reduce to normal production cost increases, leaving no room for economic profits; long the medium of Protectionists.

Tax Policy Economists claim all the above objections concern in-process short-term economic adjustments, which can be moderated in impact with Federal Resource regulation and Government supply-contract issuance to maintain economic performance. The alteration of policy would have no impact upon the Money Supply, actually increasing expandible reserves over the long-run. Consumer demand would rise, but would be met with more profitable, higher production levels over the long-run. Conglomerations would decline as Corporate managements concentrated on the profitability of current operations; demanded by the exterior financing. Bank reserves would increase by approximately forty percent, as the profitability of Corporate exterior financing began return to lending institutions. Wage demands would decline, as Companies could offer stock and higher benefits—both deductible from the tax base as Wage expense. The spread of Corporate profits predict an increase of average Household wealth by half the issued funds. This Author suggests the standard of living of Americans could rise 15%, from the increased distribution alone.

4

Historical Economic Policies

Laymen, and considerable numbers of Economists, fail to understand the differing needs for Economic performance; dependent upon previous performance, aggregation of capital, technological advance, and the magnitudes of Resources, labor, and the educational attainment of the labor force. This converts to a statement: The needs of the Economy alter with growth of size, efficiency of performance, and levels of aggregate capital. Economic policy must be designed for each level of development, because previous economic policy emphasized the needs of the Economy at the time it was first developed. Study of the American economy through it's history can provide insight.

The original American economy at the time of the Revolution was a basic Agrarian economy; supplying raw materials, food, or specialized products (Fur) to more developed societies. The Revolutionary War cut the American colonies off from the more industrialized economies of Europe. This impelled the first industrialization in American society, though it was a basic Cottage industry industrialization; providing basic household goods, agricultural implements, and shipping for these products and agricultural goods. The important criteria to be observed in this economic structure lay in the low capitalization needs. Few businesses employed more than twenty individuals, with a capital aggregation of only personal hand tools and raw materials. Business management skills, craft labor, and a source of short-term operating funds sufficed in this economy.

The movement West began to alter this Economy after 1800. The influx of population and draft of wagons, agricultural tools, and household products to be taken West, altered the craft industry of the Period into lines of modern business. Higher necessary output insisted on more laborers per business, specialization at specific task because of higher personal skill, and stockpiling of component parts. All required great Plant, with storage facilities for inventory and for finished product until sold. Labor required larger work areas, for use of expanded specialized personal tools and labor-saving machinery (Block and tackle assemblies, work tables, etc.). The greater Plant insisted upon higher capitalization, the introduction of basic maintenance expense, and larger payrolls and operating funds.

The Period between 1800–1820 brought the first organized agricultural product processing plants, along with advanced Sawmills and transfer of smithy to metalworks. Barrels of Pork started to leave the States for the markets of Europe, in addition to finished Masts, Spars, and Sheet Canvas. European orders for shipping started to arrive at American Shipyards. The American economy suddenly needed a Money Supply four times it's original size. The first National Bank system was organized, with massive inputs of investment capital from Europe; coming in by Immigrant holdings, and Continental merchant accounts in the United States. The American economy grew rapidly.

The Southern Plantation system was functionally mature by the end of 1820. Extensive material has been written of the evils of this system; but economically, it possessed an agricultural efficiency which was not surpassed until the 1960s. Massive amounts of European specie traveled to the United States, paying for the intensive production of agricultural produce which the plantation system drew from the ground. Many claim the Southern Planter class squandered the wealth in personal products and pleasures. Actual fact indicates the Plantation system paid for the infrastructure necessary for the movement West for all of the Country, through tariffs and taxes assessed on the Southern exports and imports. This included Roads, Canals, bridging, shipping, and military forces. The Northern concentration of population, during the period, led to full development of the industrial plant system of manufacture; fed by raw materials from the West and South. The West adopted most of the characteristics of the North and South, and began the third great source of commerce of the United States; the river traffic over the rivers to New Orleans, then transfer to Europe and the North. Industry developed quickly along the river system; fueled by capital from the North, South, and Europe.

The American Civil War propelled an industrialization in the South, due to the blockade. It caused a differentiation of industry in the West around the river system, for whom the blockade of the Mississippi by the South incited self-production of household and agricultural implement products, with co-development of the railway system. Northern manufacturers found themselves forced to develop international sources of raw materials, as they were cut off from the products of the South and West. Huge industrial growth came with the four years of the War, along with standardization of Parts, modern methods of production, and a huge need for an increase in the Money Supply. The latter was fulfilled by the second great wave of European investment in the United States, the first having started and finished in the period of 1815–1840. The second wave duration was from 1862–1890, and fueled the growth of railroads, steel mills, mines, and ranching in the United States.

The United States existed throughout the Nineteenth century without a recognizable economic policy. The Government paid it's expenses with tariffs and imposts, with the States use of property taxes; no element paying for modern community services, just basic outlays for infrastructure and national defense. Shortages of the Money Supply were capitalized by extensive foreign investment, with a steady rate of growth. Capital aggregation was acquired by the development of the modern Corporation, and development of monopolies. Most Economists do perceive the monopolistic pricing of the Era replaced the modern system of taxation by Government, enjoining a forced Savings rate in the populace; all under the control of the Robber Barons. This can basically be seen as private management of economic policy, and it was an extreme policy of economic growth. The Economy exploded with growth in this Period from 1860 until 1905.

The first recognizable Government economic policy came with the First World War, prior to American entrance into the conflict. The huge draft of industrial capacity during the War, by Britain, France, and Canada, brought Government action; simply to regulate the great inflationary pressures caused by these nations' search for munitions and supplies. Basic allocation analysis was developed in this Period, though overt Government control was not introduced until American entrance into the War. Massive Government regulation of resources and transport began in the War. The end of the War brought the first great shock, for all concerned. All thought such regulation and economic policy was necessary only under conditions of warfare; believing normal business of peacetime could be sustained with the self-regulation of business. Huge unemployment fueled from returning Veterans alongside massive cutbacks of heavy industry with loss of munitions contracts brought Recession. Business still refused to accept Government coordination by effective economic policy.

The attitude persisted until the Great Depression, proclaimed and maintained by the business community. They had failed to understand the American economy had changed. More Americans were engaged in commerce than in Agriculture, aggregate capital had grown at a fantastic rate, with a necessary rate of return unguaranteed by unregulated market forces, and carrying a huge employee base who would not submit to subsistence wages. Much of the industrialized nations had been financially depleted by the War, and foreign investment had dried up. An Economy never before dependent upon internal capitalization of investment, needing the natural market of intense domestic Sales; found itself with neither.

Business tried to return to the Robber Baron philosophy of cheating labor out of their wages, and could not understand the loss of a Consumer market. The Federal Reserve System had been introduced in 1912, and was instrumental in funding the First Great War; but was not expected to interfere in the internal operation of local banks. The banks channeled investments to business, and ignored the arena of Personal financing. They forbade Consumer finance, and over-capitalized industry and the Stock Market. The Great Depression was inevitable!

The above great event had actually been forestalled by three factors, all generating from the same source. The source was the sustained sale of agricultural products at effective price, from the First World War through the 1920s. Most farmers of the Period would disagree, but only because of the capitalization and expenditure patterns of themselves during the Period. The First World War had destroyed European agriculture, and had on-going effects. Much land was removed from production because of the warfare upon it, or transference to the industrial and residential sectors. A huge draft of agricultural labor had been lost as casualties from the War; the remaining drifted toward the higher wages of the industrial sector, who had also lost huge numbers of labor. Traditional agricultural methods kept European agricultural labor productivity at pre-War levels. American agriculture sold huge amounts of product to the European market, until European farmers struggled to their feet; finally starting the process of technological change with a new Generation of agricultural labor by 1930.

The huge draft of American agricultural labor into the military during the War, left them with a definite impression of the advantage of mechanization. They came home to stare at their horses and wagons, and started to buy trucks and tractors. This Period before the Great Depression was the Age of Agricultural mechanization. This transfer brought additional demand for roads and bridges, and the Construction industry boomed. Automobile and Agricultural Implement companies could not keep up with demand, while new highways and streets were started daily. Laborers, paid well, bought a huge list of Consumer goods. All was paid by agricultural product sales throughout the World.

The Period was also the beginning of the modern Entertainment industry, generated by the new leisure time occasioned by mechanization of agriculture and household; paid by high wages in the booming industries and the illicit aggregation of funds from Prohibition. Hard labor ceased to be the road to riches, replaced with specialized occupation; the Service industry starting it's rise. The rise of the Middlemen began to unfold, with marketing, distribution, and advertising underwriting entertainment costs as Sales attraction. Entertainment dispersion occasioned envy of easier lifestyles, and the movement to the Cities.

Certain danger signs were already present, though; especially the lack of modernization in bank practice. Housing increased dramatically over the Period, but within the constriction of antiquated mortgage lending stipulating excessive equity and down payments. The housing of those who could afford such conditions, was quickly being built. The laborers of high wages were quickly being equipped with modern household conveniences. All production spurts of the Era consisted of intermediate or long retention goods, supplied at fantastic rates at reasonable price. The Poor still lacked this growth in the standard of living, without any viable financial instruments to fund their transfer. The Great Depression of Lack of Consumer Demand was about to hit.

The Great Depression was the direct result of a lack of Consumer Credit. Warehouses were full of intermediate goods awaiting sale. Construction began to decline with the lack of Mortgage extension. Local banks and wealthy engaged in the quick profits of the Stock Market, with decreasing funding of infrastructure and actual industry. The start of new businesses (Service, Retail, and Sector support) dropped with the transference of funds to the Stock Market. Corporations did not diversify their profits, simply reinvesting for expansion; most often investing in rising Stocks. Intermediate Goods and new housing sales became saturated with the Credit crunch, everyone had a car, and farmers had their tractors and harvest equipment. Corporation after

Corporation started to report no Sales, without Profits; dividends became a loved Ghost of yesteryear. The Stock Market turned Bear, with the shooting and butchering of the Bull!

The 1930s started with the complete loss of liquidity. The funds had disappeared with the Market crash. Banks held no equity, having invested heavily in the Market prior to the Crash. Manufacturers and Retailers thought to cut prices to generate Sales, but refused to sell at a loss; so the average price reductions were less than twenty percent of retail. Wealthy and stable- income employees refused to replace their intermediate goods at such prices; often after taking a bath in the Stock Market Crash. No Study has been conducted to the Author's knowledge, but the Crash is estimated to cost personal loss of equity for these Classes; of almost five years' income at the minimum. The Poor could not buy, as they had no source of funding; and were about to lose their current income. The first years were years of falling agricultural prices, turning to years of Crop failure; as the Great American Dust Bowl began. The European Economies had failed as well, and the rest of the World lacked technological status and integrated Utility systems; so there was nowhere to sell the excessive American product stockpiles.

Corporations reduced labor rolls, so Consumption was cut; by an estimated sixty percent over the already halved Consumption rate. Some evidence exists almost 15% of the new car production of 1930 was sold as Used Cars, after an intervening three years. Banks started to fold, as they faced their first loss in the Market; their second loss in the failures of local business. Bank depositors started to carry Shotguns to withdraw their money; it did not help, there was no money to withdraw. The Federal Government introduced it's first Income tax since the Civil War; with economic conditions and tax rates set, actually found only Seven percent of the population paying any tax. Times were real bad, and getting worse.

The Hoover administration was actually first to initiate Keynesian deficit spending, in attempts to spur the Economy. His major failure was being at the helm during the period of the Crash. Republicans ran him for President in 1932, simply because no other Republican wished to suffer such resounding defeat. The Roosevelt administration came in, vastly expanding the Keynesian precept of deficit spending. Little economic spur was derived! We now know simple Keynesian spending alone is not enough. The New Deal thought to provide subsistence income for unemployed Americans, through an array of programs. Subsistence income does not increase Consumer Demand, except for agricultural products, clothing, fuel, and housing. It would not restart industry.

Recovery from the Depression came from a number of factors, with help from Government and industry. Consumer credit extension began on an ad hoc basis. Basic Retailers like Penny's, Wards, and Sears examined their early history, and determined to allow their Customers to run monthly accounts; thinking these Customers to be basically honest, and simply adding an interest charge onto the unpaid balance. This effort was helped by Manufacturers, who started to issue Consignments on credit, repayment after retail sale; this to maintain some level of production, and maintain retail distribution systems. It started to rain once more, and farmers started to bring in agricultural surpluses. Railroads started to haul more than Hobos, as foreign trade started to pick up. The Government found World War Two looming, and started to expand the military; this gave Thousands a job in the military, and many more Thousands Consumption-building wages in the military supply industries. The most vital single component was the aging of Intermediate Goods and Housing, which dictated replacement; the old tin Lizzy had just quit! People started going off to work in the morning.

Government began heavy spending in actual industry with the advent of the Second World War. Consumer Demand immediately picked up, too fast; rationing boards were set up for the war effort. This forced a huge rate of Personal Saving, as well as created a Black Market; which may have been the most effective in existence (there is a rumor of a Latin American country buying an aircraft carrier from

Black Market sources, immediately after the War). Just an Insider joke among Economists (???). The high taxation, plus the increased personal savings, created an immensely stocked Money Supply. It dictated the economic policy immediately after the War.

Business leadership observed the better times under heavy Government expenditure in heavy industry. They forestalled a reduction of taxation on Personal Income, though they wrangled major business tax advantages. They pressured for the continuance of heavy military spending, plus keeping an extensive military force in Europe. Huge expenditures were made for national defense, with heavy emphasis on expensive, industrially-produced weapons systems. Actual identification of any Enemy is hard to define; a Study made in 1998 suggests the capacity to attack America's homeland for purposes of conquest has never existed, and none could viably be mounted by any nation before 2015. Current status of nuclear deterrence considers it would require two weeks maintenance to attain even thirty percent of declared power for the weaponry; it is not a latter-day failing of the military, simply the implication One does not leave expensive machinery age without continuous maintenance for years at a time. No one should feel frightened, almost all other nations have worse maintenance records. Still, Four trillion plus dollars has been spent on military appropriations in this Country, since 1945.

The second element establishing economic policy after the Second World War was the desolation of Europe. The American Consumer was accustomed to paying high prices for Consumer goods, what with rationing and the operation of the Black Market. Business leadership felt no desire for price reductions; given the accumulated savings of Americans, and the ability to sell in Europe. They solved the problem of Sales to Europe, through the Consumer Credit strategy of the Marshal Plan. Sales to Europe were assured, and continued high Consumer prices were justified. The economic strategy worked well for Business interests, well into the 1960s.

The American Economy faced many changes by the start of the Sixties, as well as having changed dramatically in construct. The training skills and education of American labor functionally doubled between 1945 and 1960. Well over fifty percent of labor was still agricultural or manual labor up to the end of World War II. This statistic drop to twenty percent in the fifteen next years. Industrial labor up to the Second World War remained basic machine operators, simply putting parts into a machine, and hitting the clutch. Production changed rapidly to the point where productive labor was integrated into the lowest level of Quality control. They had to perform basic Maintenance on their equipment, and were assigned production quotas for bonuses, benefits, and job retention; the latter resolved in a probationary hiring period.

The educational level speeded forward, with introduction of the G.I. Bill. The numbers of college graduates doubled, then tripled. Business and Industry expanded technologically with the superior skills of the Labor force. The production lines of old modified to become project station assembly lines, where Workers would perform multiple tasks at the slower pace of the line. The number of workers per assembly line began to decrease, while the cost of capital equipment began to increase in both dollars and percentage cost of production. Increasing numbers of blue collar workers started the migration to lowest management levels. The college graduates expanded the Middleman business sector, introducing the first great exchange cost, between production and final Retail. Middleman distribution costs rose from an estimated Five percent to almost forty percent; while the production of specialized technology products expanded by almost Seven percent per year from 1947–1965.

American business operated in an entirely different economy, than they had in 1945. Europe and Japan rebuilt their industrial base by 1960, and foreign demand for American industrial goods was declining. The American capital investment base had practically tripled in the prior fifteen years, and it supported a population of labor plus dependents which was much greater. The need for heavy returns on production continued to mount, as the Market for such production started to decline. Alteration of economy policy was needed, to meet the different economic environment.

The economic strategy adopted was the Kennedy Tax Cut and the Johnson Great Society. The Tax Cut allowed Business to produce below economic cost, though above production and marketing costs. This was done by turning the unpaid taxes into Profits. The Great Society created a new market for Consumption, by providing the Poor with the capacity to purchase as Consumers. The economic policy had a serious drawback, in providing Government Services without funding; the equivalent of Product-dumping of Government Services. Most Economists blame the Inflation of the 1970s on the Vietnam War and the 1973 Oil Embargo, but it was the excessive Government acquirement of debt which was the real culprit.

The Vietnam War was probably no more costly to the American economy, than was the Korean Conflict; in percentage terms of economic cost, given the altered magnitudes of the American economy. The Oil Embargo was only the draw which broke the camel' back, not the cause of the burden. Realistic statistics on the American economy of the time, would set the real cost increase of production to the American economy from the increased cost of fuel; at only an approximate four percent rise in production cost, with a eight percent rise in household maintenance cost. Neither Event could be expected to have caused the double digit Inflation of the 1970s. The Federal Deficit was the Evil deed!

The Supply-Side Economists with alliance with the Monetarists came to power with the Reagan administration. They claimed the Kennedy Tax Cut had been right and good, and the Johnson Great Society wrong. Their economic policy and formula for success was more tax cuts for business, relaxation of Credit terms for investment, and sharp restriction of Government spending; but only on welfare programs, not on Government contracts to business which needed purported increase. The American economy headed into what will be called the Great Mini-Depression of Reagan someday.

Consumer demand started to plummet, while Consumer debt started to skyrocket. The standard of living for the Poor started to drop at three percent per year, until it had fallen by a third. The term Working Poor was coined, to define those who worked, but whose income was still at the poverty level; percentages of this functionally new class going from an originating five percent to a functional forty percent of the blue collar class by 1993. Huge investment was derived from the relaxation of Credit restrictions; most of which were unsound, due to the lack of Consumer consumption, and almost total lack of collateral equity for these loans. Businesses were started by Individuals with equity of only a house with a twenty year mortgage, soon claiming to have a net worth of Five million; and searching for new investment loans. What followed was the S&L Bailout, and the crippling of the banking industry. The Federal Debt grew, as did the Inflation rate.

The real turnaround came with the Clinton administration, causation having absolutely nothing to do with the previous administration policies; though Republicans like to claim it was Reagan policies which produced the Boom of the 1990s. Any Economist will state economic initiatives work within three years of implementation, else they do not work; the Reagan initiatives expressed themselves in the S&L Bailout and mounting Federal Debt. The Clinton initiatives were to cut military spending, limit growth of the Federal Civil Service plus it's benefits packages, and actually negotiate Federal supply contracts. All efforts aided the slowing of accumulation of National Debt and the Inflation rate, but it was not enough.

The identifiable turning point was the 1993 Tax Increase. The Reagan Tax Cut was erased, business went back to paying taxes, Capital gains was again being effectively taxed, and the wealthy Ten percent of the Nation was again paying an equitable share of the tax burden. The tax burden of the Middle Class actually increased, but certain observable trends could be observed. The Consumer Debt of the Middle Class almost immediately started to decrease. The ranks of the Working Poor started to decline, as their income rose above the poverty line. Lending institutions immediately began to show enhanced Profits. The Federal Government slowly gained revenues, until it showed a surplus in 1997. Business started to expand from the Profits of increased Consumer numbers in the market. The Recipients of Capital Gains were showing higher after-tax revenues, than they had shown of before-tax revenues when they had not been paying taxes. Observance of the Time suggests a Six percent shift of tax burden upward, produced a Sixteenth percent increase in the standard of living overall.

Economists demand explanation for this economic gain. The answer is relatively simple. Wealthy classes spend only about thirty percent of their Income in actual Consumption; the rest is re-invested, or transferred to dependents in forms which cannot be spent. Middle Class Incomes spend about 65% of their income as Consumption, lower Middle Class incomes spend about seventy percent of their income as Consumption. Working Class spend almost 85% of their income as Consumption. Working Poor spend 97% of their Income as Consumption. Each class of Income spends any increase in Income at the same approximate rate. Each class of Income cuts their expenditures at approximately one-half the rate of their Income loss. The Income gainers by the 1993 Tax Cut exceeded the Income losers by about 70 to 1. Consumer demand increased by about 11% per year between 1994 and 2000. It was good for Business!

Trouble started to loom for the American Economy, with the functional Republican takeover of Congress in 1994. The Democrats held them off for a considerable number of years, but Tax law of 1998, 99, and 2000 started to replace tax credits for Business and the Rich. They were able to shift about three percent of the tax burden downward once more, even before the leave-taking of Bill Clinton. Business profits immediately started to suffer, as Consumer demand dropped. This is the Period when Corporate leadership started to hide loss of profitability, through the building of Corporate debt.

The entrance of the Bush administration (the Younger) had almost immediate economic impact. Price increases on Government supply contracts with Business went up twenty percent almost from Day One of the Bush administration. The Republican Congress expanded it's own budget by forty percent, in the first month. Eighty percent of military weaponry and infrastructure contracts with Business were rubber-stamped, at the prices requested of the supplying businesses. The Federal Government can be estimated to have been spending in deficit condition, prior to the Bush Tax Cut; which rolled back tax rates to the Reagan Tax Cut, with added advantages for Corporations. The total downward shift of the Tax burden, from earlier Cuts and the Bush Tax Plan, can be estimated as almost Eight percent. Then came the disaster of September 11th.

The idea the Federal Deficit is caused by the War on Terrorism stands as a false claim. Total economic percentages of the money spent, considering the magnitudes of the two different economies, indicates the War on Terrorism is less costly than the Korean War in economic terms. An estimated Four percent Surtax on Income, as compared to Ten percent Surtax during the Vietnam War, could pay for the War on Terrorism. The Federal Deficit is caused by a failure to tax, nothing else!

The shift of the tax burden downward, plus increasing Government deficit, shows immediate impact on the Economy. Consumer demand indicates a rate of drop of Eight percent from 2000. Increase of Consumer debt to total income expresses a growth rate of Three percent per year, since the increased tax on lower incomes from 1998. Health care insurance for Workers is discontinued at Four percent per year, while Health Care provision costs increase at a double-digit rate; 95% of this increase coming from business price increases on medical supplies, equipment, and Drugs. Business product prices have shown indication of a Three percent rise per year in all Corporate-produced products since 1999, while Personal Income has been rising at a scant One percent per year. Inflation estimates are being falsified by Government, through continual alteration of the Product mix evaluated. The actual National Deficit can be expected to exceed Government claims by a least four to one. Estimates of Economic Growth must be considered suspicious at best, with the drop of Consumer Demand clearly present.

The Reader must grasp one essential element of economic policy. It exists whether there is a defined policy present, or not. The absence of economic policy is, in itself, an economic policy. The Economy functions, and production continues, no matter what economic policy is in force. The profitability of that economic function constitutes the desires of defined economic policy. The Economy contains such a range of operation, though, economic policy can often possess absolutely counter-productive effects on profitability; as was the goal of the policy. Advantages to Business may not increase business performance. Advantages to Consumers may not increase Consumption. Greater Government expenditures may not increase total production. The Economist has learned to live with this frustration, which may take months of economic activity, only to learn an economic initiative had a counter-productive effect. The Layman has not. The context of debate, and the interplay of initiative, would almost be comic relief; except for the fact, all affect the Incomes and lifestyle of all operating in the Economy under study.

5

Keynesian Theory

John Maynard Keynes was probably the first great Economist in the modern sense; evaluating the procedural elements of economic performance. There is no detriment which can diminish his contribution to the field of Economics. His condemnation of the 1919 Versailles Treaty ending the First World War, led to the first concrete studies of aggregation of capital and Investment return. His work of the 1920s advanced theory on Trade balances. He identified Government as the major Participant of any Economy, due to it's taxation, provision of civil services, and national defense. It contains the sorrow of all great Men, Keynes finds greatest remembrance for a theory holding essential flaws.

Keynes basically argued Government should make up for shortfalls of Consumer Demand, by greater participation in the market. This effort should consist of deficit spending with reduction of taxation, so as not to further injure Consumer Demand. He wrote extensively on the subject, but this was the gist of his argument. Government was to generate economic performance through it's own action as Consumer (and Employer) in the market. His major problem was lack of differentiation of the types of Government expenditure; thinking simple expenditure of any type would raise Consumption. Actual statistical evaluation has since proven this assumption false.

Labor initially seized upon this doctrine, embellishing it as rationale for the welfare system. The Great Depression drew Business to it's support, as potential nostrum for the total lack of viable rates of production. Government after Government adopted programs of varying degrees of adherence to the perceived Keynesian doctrine. Study of economic history highlights almost all such programs failed, except in Nazi Germany. These failures came from basic flaws in the thought of Keynes, the success of Nazi Germany came from their variance from basic Keynesian structure. Nazi Germany first entered the Arms Race to rearm from the disastrous disarmament provisions of the Versailles Treaty of 1919, providing Consumer Demand creating employment based on high Wages issued to munitions industry labor and construction workers on the Autobahn..

Keynesian theory fails because it does not refine Government participation in the market. Simple Government spending may or may not induce economic revitalization. The key to success comes from a series of limitations inherent in the operation. The first and paramount restriction comes in the level of economic activity. The second restriction insists expenditures must increase Consumer Demand, not simply production. The third restriction insists the draft of resources must not curtail Consumer Demand through Inflation. All will be considered.

Boom economic conditions actually possess a production rate which utilizes a capital equipment usage greater than 71%. Bear economic conditions express a capital utilization rate which drops below 66% (actually based only on a two-shift, 40 hour Week production level). Investment and recapitalization rates drop off when the capital utilization rate fall below 66%. They decrease by ten percent, for every point drop in the utilization rate past this point; until Investment is zero, and recapitalization is only twenty percent of replacement value, real contraction of the Economy occurring through capital equipment aging. The Author must mention here, there is considerable contestation of these numbers. Full pattern studies in the area suffer from universal application (conflicting data pressures), or errors in data compilation.

Keynesian theory value loss comes from the fact Government participation cannot fund Investment and recapitalization above the normal

Production rates. There is no economic fuel from Government expenditures, if the capital utilization rate exceeds 71% by whatever amount of funds spent above this rate. The Government expenditures fuels only Investment and recapitalization Costs, leaving Consumer Demand unaffected. Actual studies indicate the effect of Consumer Demand stays indifferent, if Government expenditures are spent anywhere there is a capital utilization rate above 66%. The Government only adds production by the value of the expenditure, but does not affect the decisions of either Business or Consumers. Serious impact of simple Keynesian theory comes only when the capital utilization rate is below 60%, where it directly fuels recapitalization. This will not fuel any economy growth, unless tied to Consumer Demand creation initiatives.

Consumer Demand must be expanded to actually fuel an economy. All Governments failed in their welfare programs in the 1930s, except for Nazi Germany. This entity insisted on rebuilding national armaments plus building the Autobahn system for military transportation. They paid top price for this production, and workers derived Consumption-increasing wages from the work. The German economy thrived. Other Governments starved because they thought only to provide subsistence welfare (Consumption increasing, but not Consumer Demand increasing), and waited until the Armaments race to provide top wage work by Government expenditure. The Great Depression started to end with this Consumption-increasing fuel, though the sale of Intermediate Goods had started to pick up previously..

The third restriction is harder to define, with much argument by most Economists. Everyone can agree Inflation will negate Government expenditures to fuel the economy, because Inflation curtails Consumption. Most will agree Government deficit spending increases the inflation rate of resource pricing by some percentage. They agree inflation in the resource market leads to inflation throughout the economy, with relatively no suppressive measures to be implemented. Most Economists demur at the suggestion the magnitudes of Government

expenditure produce sufficient Inflation to make appreciable difference, as these magnitudes rarely exceed levels of Full Production
resource consumption The exact impact on inflation pricing of Government deficit spending brings argument in exact definition.

This Author has found every dollar of Government deficit spending
costs a $.0274 rise in resource prices. This means a 100 billion dollar
deficit will produce a 2.74 billion dollar increase in resource prices. It's
impact holds importance because it rarely furthers follow-up production, as does even Consumer consumption. This translates as Government expenditure does not fund future production. The Economy
stands as a circular process, with the end-process funding and fueling
the initial production. Government expenditure removes assets from
the Economy to limit the production process, even in welfare transfer
payments for Consumption; this Consumption not labor payment to
the production process. The resource inflation from Government
spending therefore is a direct reduction of production.

The Government currently claims the deficit is 158 billion dollars,
and is to the Author's mind, lying as to the magnitude of the deficit.
Residual long-term impact of inflation on the total market from inflation on the resource market is debatable: economic estimates ranges
from $.30 for every resource market dollar increase, to $7 in overall
inflation, for every dollar of resource market inflation. Importance
comes from actual increase in the numbers of dollars spent on end-
product units; reflecting unit production cost increase, not increased
production levels. This complete action, though, has an approximate
three-year delay, though the effect on the resource market is almost
immediate; interim overall inflation building at steady rates determined by pressure on resources throughout industries.

Return to study of Keynesian theory would state there are limitation
to economic fuel by Government deficit spending. There will be only
an adverse effect of this spending, if the capital equipment utilization
rate is above 66%; due to inflation in the resource market. Study of the
resource market inflation suggests there will be no elimination of Infla-

tion due to Government deficit expenditure, until resource stockpiles exceed twelve percent. A measurable indicator with some relevance (at least to the Author) portrays a necessary production for 2.34 years at levels of 66% of the capital equipment utilization level, to generate a stockpile of resources in excess of twelve percent. This means a Bear economy must operate for over two years before Government deficit spending becomes economic fuel. Any Government deficit expenditure must be spent on paying Consumption-increasing wages, if there is to be any economic fuel at all.

The real problem of Keynesian deficit spending to fuel the economy lies in it's refusal to die. Supply-Side and Monetarist Economics both integrate Keynesian deficit spending into their own calculations to improve performance. No wealth of economic data contradicting the effects of deficit spending, professed by themselves, seems to make any difference. Supply-Siders insist any increase of production is good for business, therefore good for the economy. The Monetarists acclaim the additional funds provided by Government, discounting the real generation of inflation. Supply-Siders see no reason to differentiate Government expenses for best economic performance, as long as the funds wind up in the hands of business. Monetarists only wish for increases in the Money Supply.

The real truth remains Government deficit spending provides real economic fuel under only Depression conditions, or Recession conditions lasting longer than 2.34 years in duration. It will work then, only if the funds are used for infrastructure construction or national defense; both industries with Consumption-increasing wages. This is a much different proscription than high Government expenditures paid by Taxation, anathema for Supply-Siders. This will be studied in a later Chapter.

[Author's Note: Some level of welfare transfer payments must be engaged, because Consumer Demand will suffer, as will the Labor Supply. Some Studies express preference for such levels being less than infrastructure payments, because Consumer Demand pressure negate production expansion from infrastructure construction. This becomes a very important argument in the discussion of Medicare and medical insurance by Private Insurers. The universality of medical care extension expresses a huge expenditure which consists of heavy welfare transfer payments. A direct Labor purchase of such medical care would bring a forty percent reduction of such medical care. Sixty percent of such medical care concerns excessive testing, pricing, and treatments without relative degree of success. The Whole vastly skews the performance of the Economy.]

6

Supply-Side Economics

The Supply-Side Economist holds 'Aggregation of Capital' as his God, and woe to those who would disagree. They believe business has not only the right, but the duty, to concentrate assets for investment. It remains a tenant of the religion, any means possible are to be used, even to the point of tax evasion. They insist Government leave business free to acquire these investment assets, free of intrusion and the devil of taxes. The latest Bush Tax Plan actually gets into the Corporate welfare system, granting tax rebates to business; which had never been paid in the first place. Supply-Side Economics is in the ascendency, but not for long; due solely to poor economic performance.

Study of the process of capital aggregation relates differing realities from the Supply-Side model. Almost all successful new businesses are externally-financed from lending institutions; having provided a Prospectus of specific detail, to satisfy picky bankers. A review of these successful startups would indicate almost an eighty percent fulfillment of the specifics of the Prospectus. Almost every business of this type show extended finance for the goal of expanding the specifics of the Prospectus, because of discovered markets. This extended finance invariably came from a lending institution, who express quicker exploitation of market advantage, than do separate business entities of duration. These financial institutions also show quicker response rates than do Corporations who use Buyout performance, to acquire added operations. The slowness and restriction of external financing is hard to find.

Estimates by the Author place a seventy percent higher profitability on Operations, originally funded by lending institution; who force management to consider all aspects of reducing costs, advertising dollar advantage per market venue, expansion into new markets, and proper recapitalization rates for expansion. Lending institutions insist on proper business conduct from management, and complete financial accounting according to accepted lending institution rules. The lending institutions force realistic rates of expansion, based on Sales estimates derived by market analysis. Contrary to the suggestions of Supply-Side Economists claiming lack of possible exploitation of profitability, lending institutions outline greater concentration to the bottom line, than does either Corporate Board or Stockholders.

Business originate operating a specialty, either producing specific product, or providing specific service. Expansion comes to exploit new markets, or to absorb excess Profits from operations. The first entails only expansion of the specialty, of which Management possesses expertise. The second brings change of operational direction, where Management does not have experience. The development of alternate expertise can be learned, but only at the halving of supervision by Management over all operations. Profits will drop directly with the drop of supervision; either through the necessary acquisition of additional supervisory personnel, or distraction from cost-saving initiatives. Owners, or Management and Stockholders, would invariably find outside investment superior in profit returns, all market discontinuities eliminated.

Corporate Buyouts by Parent company stock issuance and payment always show a drop of Buyout profitability of operation, due to disturbance of Management personnel, expansion of operations with lowered production rates, and higher marketing costs. This comes at a time of needed increased Profitability, due to the increased issuance of stock. Internally-financed product line startups stand as difficult to quantify, because of Corporation withholding of records; but the Author estimates new production line startups from internal-financing are two to three times as costly as are externally-financed production line startups. This results from pre-established wage scales for management and possibly labor, utilization of pre-existent supply contracts rather than the open market, and dispersal of marketing assets. Internally-financed additions of product lines, in both cases, average much higher operating costs for the Parent company, and delayed returns for the product line.

Supply-Side Economists oppose excessive dispersal of Profits to Stockholders on the claim this disperses capital formation. The above argument outlines clearly Stockholders could more profitably invest such funds in outside investment, clearly a greater aggregation of capital and Profits; than the Corporation can possibly manage. The advantage of this distribution would be an average rise of a guessed 11% of the Consumer Demand ratios of Stockholders. They would claim this is a dispersal of aggregated capital, but it would increase the profitability of invested capital; leading to increased investment. The economic term for this states: The increased flow of capital funds will increase the speed of business transactions, leading to more rapid realization of Profits; inciting a faster investment and savings rate.

Any discussion of tax incentives for business must enter study of Supply-Side Economics. It has already been established earlier that a shift of tax burden upward, increases Consumer Demand faster than loss of income; shift of tax burden downwards reduces Consumer demand faster than gain of Income. Business remains the richest element in any economy; shifting tax weight off of business will actually reduce Business consumption for Economic Growth; because of reduced Consumer Demand, caused by tax burden shifted to personal consumers. Reduced Business tax burden actually reduces Production and economic performance, as production schedules are cut because of reduced demand for product.

An icon of Supply-Siders stands as elimination of the Capital Gains Tax; they claim it is a double tax on business profits, and counterproductive. The analogy is stupid! Payments from one entity to another remains a cost to the one, and income to the other. It remains equivalent of stating a worker should not be liable to tax, because his Employer pays tax on his income. Or Business need not pay a tax, because other businesses he deals with, and his Customers, pay their income tax. The reality stands Capital Gains is Income to a distinct entity, income separate as an award for investment capital; unconnected to the Issuer. Further reality states personal Income earners who do not pay their share of the income tax, reduce the Consumption of those who do pay their Income tax. Corporation Income taxes must be defined as payment of infrastructure costs for doing business, with no suggestion this is not legitimate expense. Elimination of the Capital Gains tax would actually bring a shift of the tax burden downward of almost Seven percent, leading to a reduction of estimated Consumer Demand in excess of fifteen percent.

Their last great desire is for the elimination of the Inheritance Tax. They back this claim with the assertion such elimination would further aggregation of capital, and enhance economic performance. This is patently false! Statistics state every additional award of one million dollars to an heir brings a 17% heir reduction in economic production labor. It increases a parasite class, whose expenditure pattern cuts the incentive package advantage for working. Inheritance awards of magnitude actually reduce entrepreneurship, as heirs shift operational burdens of ownership to paid employees, with definable reductions in profitability. The elimination of Inheritance tax would reduce Consumer Demand by an estimated eight percent, as the tax burden was again shifted downwards. Actual reduction of Capital Aggregation would incur, to the tune of the full value of Consumption derived from unearned Income. Vast inheritance awards create a wastrel class, to the great detriment of the labor force and economy.

Supply-Side Economists advocate for the One-Percent class of Wealthy in this Country. This class would like to increase their holdings, reduce their taxes, and pass on their power over the economy to their heirs. Their operational conduct reduces Consumer Demand, runs the Government at a deficit which ordinary taxpayers must pay, and actually cuts the profitability of lending institutions. There is no evidence existent that tax credits for Business actually increases economic investment or performance, as Profits are shifted to pay for unprofitable operations or personal aggrandizement for business leadership; under the spectrum of sharply curtailed Consumer Demand. Supply-Siders are on top of current discussion of economic policy; but cannot claim leadership in any Growth period, and have not had a successful report to date.

[Author's Note: Laymen may have some difficulty in understanding the impact of the tax burden shift downward of the Supply-Side theory. The award of each million dollars of Inheritance without taxation probably costs a loss of $30,000 of Consumer consumption, as lower Incomes would purchase this amount in excess of what Inheritors do consume; for each and every remaining year of the Heir's own life. The current Tax Package reducing Business taxes probably cost $17 of lost Consumption, for every dollar of Business profit gain. Realize these are only Author estimates, unbacked by statistical data.]

7

The Monetarists.

The Monetarists stand as a major trend in Economics, with their influence resting on two fundamental elements: extremely accurate statistical analysis concerning the Money Supply, and highly effective economic incentives when innate Consumer Demand is existent. They simply cannot be discounted, because of their superior methodology and excellent predictions under normal market conditions. Their only fault lay in their concentration on the Money Supply, liquidity, and the signs of Inflation. These Studies would be sufficient, if the economy always operated under normal market conditions. Skew of statistical readings appear with the generation of abnormal market conditions, for which the Monetarists lack a curative program.

They immediately insist on definition of the term abnormal market conditions. One must first state We do not operate in a free market, something which is actually an abnormal market condition. The only potential free market left consists of raw agricultural products, but the Government successfully protects American farmers from the consequences of a free market. Simply put: a free market is simply too Darwinist to provide a format in which economic opportunity can be exploited. Short-run Cost and Price crises inhibit long-run economic potentials. Business must survive in order for Profits from scale production and technological development to be attained. Advocates of a totally free market should be careful of what they wish for, getting it could destroy them.

There must be an Insurer of last resort, who will underwrite short-term failures. The base level for American business consists of Chapter 11 Bankruptcy. This allows Business to reorganize, and acquire new loans; through a Court-sponsored rationalization of their debt payment. This is the last step, but there are many other Government initiatives: Government loans or loan underwriting, Government purchase of excess product, Government excuse of tax burden, Government award of tax advantages, Government payment of Research and Development Costs, and Government payment of certain resource costs. Such efforts separate Our economy from the free market, and Business would scream at loss of this protection.

Free markets demand Production below Cost, when there is over-supply of Product. They demand Price above the normal Consumer Demand curve, in the face of acute shortage. They preclude shifts of Cost forward, due to limitations of credit extension; this through lengthened debt repayment schedules which are unprofitable. Private banks, unsupported by a Government support system, would not extend this credit. Government would not reschedule infrastructure development to aid business development. There would be unregulated supply of basic services: Power, Transportation, Communication, and Labor access routes. A free market is the ideal which no one actually wants.

The Great Depression was the prime example of Government failure to interact with the economy. There was no attempt by Government to defray or delay the costs of firms, suffering under shrunk Consumer Demand ratios. The Federal Reserve System extended neither essential business operating loans, or established the framework for adequate Consumer finance. The bankruptcy laws were barbaric, and totally antiquated for a modern economic system. Government policy insisted on supply contracts at reduced Profits for Business, or below Cost. The adoption of Keynesian policy by Roosevelt brought only subsistence payments, fueling neither Consumer Demand or Business profits. The American economy survived in spite of the Government.

Drop to free market conditions because of Government inaction (or inappropriate counterproductive action) continues as abnormal market condition, with greater threat today than believed. Another abnormal market condition resides in an artificial resource constriction, such as Crop failure, processing failure (ex. Concrete or Computer chips) of component parts, in-line hyperinflation due to mining failure or monopoly action, artificial product price inflation due to in-line profit-taking during production, and over-sale of ownership through over-supply of financial paper—diluting Profits across an inflated spectrum.

Monetarists do not adequately examine the entire Production process for magnified Costs, which can distort normal market conditions. They assume natural Cost and Price analysis to operate continually in the economic function of Production, and concentrate solely on market forces which would constrict Consumer or Business credit. They dismiss the effects of oligarchical price-setting in it's most destructive area of operation—resource mining and component supply markets. They refer to such Costs as middleman costs, implying these costs are normal business practice; therefore, actual increase in economic performance, due to increased salaries and Consumption. This is the failure of Monetarist economics!

Oligarchical price-setting in the resource and component supply markets constitute at least twenty percent of the cost of all products sold in the United States. A Shop maintenance head and the Author once calculated it would cost 8.5 times the original Sale price of a lathe, to build it from ordered parts—even if all Parts were shipped at the same time. Component parts for further production have far less markup, only between 40–200% of Production cost of the component. This is called in-line profit-taking, and translate into direct decline of final Consumer Demand. When the prices paid by Business have endured such oligarchical prices, profits of production are shifted from the hands of Labor, going directly to Business managements.

Supply-Side Economists and many Monetarists would attribute this to be beneficial. It could not be farther from the truth. Wages of Labor as percentage of total profit from production has been dropping since the Kennedy Tax Cut of 1963. The Dividends paid to Stockholders has not increased appreciably during the period. The expansion of Corporate stock has ballooned during the Period, with an increasing share of such Corporate stock being sold by Management, for the benefit of Management. Actual issuance of stock through Sale by the Corporation for corporate revenues has been declining during the Period, except in the area of newly-chartered Companies. Buyouts contains the last major issuance of stock, with the management of the purchased Company getting the lion's share of the total Parent Company dispersion of stock.

Corporate and Business managements can be estimated to acquire Sixty percent of all Business profitability in this Country today, through salaries, benefits, retirement packages, and exercise of Stock Options. Business rhetoric proclaims the purchase of Stock as the means to acquire wealth no matter the level of Dividends, through the increase of Stock prices. This allows for the easy sale of Stock, after exercising Stock Options.

The individual Stockholder should examine the equation presented, for a relative lack of truth. Examination of the history of Stock values over long periods presents a rate of growth in Stock pricing to be relatively modest, about eight percent for overall Stock price average increase since the 1970s, when considering the Mean high and lows of Stock price. Stock Splits were basically abandoned in the 1970s, when Corporations used stock issuances to reduce their Stock price. Management exercises Stock Options today along with Buyout issuances, and Share prices remain basically stabilized. Stockholders lose Share value with every Buyout or Stock Option issued, with loss of Stock price.

A forced distribution of Profits would have provided almost 18% per year Dividend over the Period, if the Profits had been distributed (this only a loose estimate, based solely on base information of unit profitability and magnitude of Sales over the Period). The Stockholder of 1980 who bought stock and held it throughout without further investment, can expect to have not yet recouped his investment; with Stock price within forty percent of his original purchase price. Forced distribution of Corporate profits would assuredly have recouped the Stockholder twice the price of the Stock, and probably four to five times that amount. This included the Corporate cost of taxes, but not Capital Gains for Stockholders.

Most would at this point suggest the Author had drifted far from criticism of Monetarist theory, so he must rectify by showing relationship. Monetarists claim Consumer Demand is only a function of the extension of Consumer credit. Consumer Demand consists of both the income of Consumers and the extension of Credit to them. The level of Credit, itself, is limited to the income earning potential of the Consumer. Corporate constriction of Dividends can be estimated to have reduced the average income of Households by some 16% percent per year. The average percentage of this lost Income which would have been used in Consumption stands at about forty percent, as most of the added income would have went to upper Middle Class and wealthy people. Corporate retention of Profits therefore reduced Consumer Demand by at least Seven percent per year since 1963. Consideration of the extension of Consumer Credit expects a two hundred percent increase in present levels, considering the added income of Households.

Monetarists do not attack the two primary retardants of economic performance: oligarchical profits-taking in the resource and component supply markets, and the non-dispersal of Corporate Profits in Dividends. They also join with Supply-Side Economics in the call to shift the tax burden downward, which again reduces Consumption greater in amounts of Sales, than the original tax credits. We are now entering into a Consumer Demand crunch, which will not be eased by loosened Consumer credit with lower interest payments. Consumers need a real increase in their disposable income, which only a tax burden shift upward could bring. We have returned to the abnormal market conditions caused by bad Government economic policy.

The last component of the Chapter should be an actual definition of normal market conditions, an attempt which will draw much amusement. Normal market conditions retain as many definitions as there are Authors of economic studies. One Economist, trying to be a Comedian, suggested any markets where profit-taking did not absorb more than Sixty percent of the Retail prices. Another advanced a theory each factor of production (Land, Labor, Capital, Transport, Distribution, and Marketing) should derive the same profit according to it's level of capitalization. A Third gives a convoluted formulation which basically said a profit spread where the unit cost of resources for production did not increase, because of successful expansion of growth and technology. A Fourth proclaims each factor of production must have equalized ratios of Investment capitalization. Does any of this tell Anyone anything?

Normal market conditions exist where Consumer Demand is met without abnormal distortion of the Household budgeting sequence. Sounds as bad as the previous, doesn't it? It can be simplified, though possibly not by the Author. Household budgeting operates on an allocation system in which every budget sector enjoys percentage Means which do not vary beyond three percent at any Period. Aberrant allocation increases will return to a basic Mean within three years, due to market response to Labor demands. It does not matter what market force or resource suddenly increased in price, nor does the largesse of such increase matter; the Market will adjust all expenses appropriately within the time period. The inability to adjust back to these Household budgetary means insist on the presence of abnormal market conditions. Many Economists would claim the Economy has never operated under normal market conditions, using this formulation; yet, it must be considered the only true test of normal market condition.

[Author's Note: The above discussion was somewhat simplified, not fully outlining Monetarist position; relatively undescribable to common Readers. The basic trouble comes from reportage influences, which though in error; lay hidden inside of Economic models, which display good readouts, but lacking real economic viability. Layman understanding may be gained by statement that Monetarist theory provides a direct loss of Consumer Demand through Credit extension payments, these interest payments returning to a fictional lender who did not actually lend anything; utilizing Consumer debt payments to fund Credit extension. Truth states such Credit extension is reduced, if Consumer debt payments reduce; increases if such payments increase. Credit extension companies purchase of operating capital credit of their own, does not mean any consumption. Consumer Credit interest payments are a direct reduction of Consumer Demand.]

8

Flawed Government Economic Policies

F.A. Hayek was a brilliant man and eminent Economist, who was resurrected by the Supply-Side Economists to counteract the Keynesian and Monetarists. His basic thesis remained information for Productive decisions could not be collated for central planning. This information was derived from a vast decentralized productive system, with correspondent decision-making at location. Any central planning had to operate on suppositions which did not account for variances at the point of production. Hayek held this factor destroyed the capacity of central planning to produce at levels common to decentralized economies. He contended no basic formulations could be found, as contretemps the Monetarists' posits, which could possibly maintain economic performance as well as the Market.

Conservative Economists use Hayek's thesis as defense in their search to remove Government economic policy from the Market. They ignore the real fact Government non-intervention constitutes a very dangerous economic policy. Non-intervention allows for corruption of products, deception in advertising, evasion of debt, inhumane work conditions, pollution of environment, and common fraud. They state they would retain this intervention by Government agencies, but want to eliminate Government intrusion, which restricts natural market forces. They are always somewhat hazy in description of these restrictions, knowledgeably fearful of public reaction to such delineation. They try to suppress the actual fact Consumer desire for product quality insists on production cost increases, and their supposed 'freedom from intrusion' consists of the right to deny Consumer preferences in pursuit of Profits.

They currently seek legislation removing the necessity of business to fully account for their charges on Consumer bills. Utilities and Telecom industries are currently privatizing their accounts from Public scrutiny, Consumers allowed to see only general charge amounts; one well-known Internet Server already charges a four percent profitability expense. They have already acquired immunity from presenting Profitability accounts, where the Profits were earned outside the taxing authority's jurisdiction. They seek to hide accounts recording the distribution of Profits from operations, information already functionally withheld from Stockholders. They have already achieved legislation allowing transfer of billing receipts outside of taxing authority jurisdiction. They increasingly reduce Government taxing of Profits, by lobbying a very corrupt Congress. Examination of the listed direction of business desire to eliminate Government intervention, suggests business seeks personal enrichment, not superior economic performance in these efforts.

Economic performance remains a multi-function, multi-variable complex of equations; which can only be simplified by the pricing mechanism. Economic size alters the matrix of equations. All the above endeavors hold as root justification for implementation of the aggregation of capital as the primary determinant of economic performance. Previous analysis expressed inefficiency of business internal financing, unfettered by strict accounting procedure. This analysis will try to indicate the simple aggregation of capital through business is more inefficient, than capital aggregation through financial institutions.

Normal market conditions operate on Supply and Demand curves which are unaffected by other motivations than Production. Efficient Supply curves consist of production costs, plus marketing and distribution costs. These costs include a normal entrepreneurial profit, expressed as a percentage of above costs. Profits above this percentage profit are considered to be Economic profits. Economists have never stipulated any analysis concerning the relevant value of this percentage profit, and will undoubtedly refrain from such speculations.

The Author believes this lack of study is great cause for inefficiencies of economic performance. His rudimentary examination assures excess profit-taking in product production constricts Consumption. Wild estimates, based mainly on intuition and some study of markets, enforces a belief any profit-taking above twelve percent per year of the combined costs will constrict Consumer consumption. This venue can best be evaluated in dollar for dollar comparison. The Author believes every dollar of Profits earned above a normal entrepreneurial Profit of twelve percent per year of combined Costs, will inflict a $2.30 reduction of Consumer consumption.

[Author's Note: The minimum twelve percent per year of combined Costs is the basic payment level for Management and Capital. Levels less than this cannot fund debt service and recapitalization, along with Management costs. Much debate exists among Economists as to the relationship between external financing and Sock ownership, most claiming there is distinct differences. The Author believes interest payments do not differ in any way from Stock dividends, and therefore; all are debt service.]

Normal Economic analysis would attribute this potential reduction a good thing, the transfer of resources from Consumption to capital formation. This argument, though, holds validity only in early industrial economies. Developed economies, like the United States, the EEU, and Japan, must maintain a minimum standard of living, in order to generate proper levels of production. Their Capital intermix is of such development and range, capital formation concerns only the percentage use of resource recovery equipment; actually only producing fuller use of said equipment, and inciting higher Profits for the industry. Economists must search elsewhere to find justification for such reductions of Consumer Demand.

Financial institutions do not aggregate capital, as does business. They simply hold and utilize temporarily unused capital assets of Consumers, during the period of this non-use. They will return the capital upon demand of the Consumer, knowing such demand can be estimated and supplied with temporary cash funds. They make their money on the efficient utilization of these unused funds, during the period of their non-use. Their charge to the Consumers are minor, and often provide profit to the Consumer. The only reduction to Consumer Demand comes from interest charges on Consumer debt and mortgages issued to the Consumer; actually effecting the utilization of temporary storage of Capital..

The greatest capability shown by financial institutions comes in direct increase of capital aggregation, with the increase of economic performance. More and higher Consumer Demands represent more deposits of increasing frequency being made in financial institutions; their Reserves growing under economic performance. They also enjoy the capacity to underwrite greater business investments, under a scenario of decreasing Consumer prices; as Consumer debt reduces in largesse, with a higher loan fulfillment ratio. Financial institutions, under the developed economy matrix, hold the capacity to handle the capital expansion of business, handle Consumer needs, and provide the filtering accounting to assure business investment is sound.

Business internal financing stands as more costly than financial institution underwriting, operates with less attention to Costs reductions and with less profitability, and is governed by refusal to distribute Profits or pay taxes. It requires the creation of an economic profit from existing Sales of currently produced product, and must have negative impact upon Consumer Demand. It functionally retards economic performance, through operation of abnormal market conditions. This reduces the standard of living of Consumers by an estimated twenty percent.

The reduction of the standard of living must be examined further, as the reduction of Consumption acts as a regressive tax upon the Poor.

Internal financing of Corporations reached it's height with the Reagan administration. The period does not start the drop of Population in America into lower economic classes according to Income; this had started after passage of the Kennedy Tax Cut, a period where Corporations truly turned to internal financing. A working family could support itself through the efforts of the head of the Household working normal hours; feeding a family of four at Income levels almost equivalent to lower middle class levels. This had changed by ten years of the Kennedy Tax incentives, to where two needed to work to maintain a family of four. Neither the Vietnam War or the Oil Embargo could have induced such a change. Study of Consumer Product price rises in the Period, paying the economic profits for Corporate internal financing, shows the clear cause of work effect reduction in real pay.

The American labor force was in dire straits by the Reagan administration. Consumer price increases demanded a two-employee Household, but economic performance was not sufficient to double the employment lists of 1963. The Reagan economic initiatives worsened the situation, shifting the tax burden again downward, reducing social welfare, and loosening bank requirements for loan extension to business. A round of speculative investment was entered into. Corporations continued their internal financing by price rises on products. Vast construction was carried out, all basically dependent on huge rises in Consumer Demand. It did not show up! Consumer Debt restrictions were eased; but Consumer Demand did not increase, though Consumer Debt ballooned. The new constructions failed, as the Consumer Demand was actually less than when the Reagan administration took office; eaten up by Corporate product prices rises, and interest charges on the Consumer Debt. A third of the American population dropped out of the middle class.

The Clinton administration came in, shifted the tax burden upward, and Corporation went into Consumer financing for their own products. They still found Consumer Demand was only present under Sale conditions, i.e., the economic profits removed from the product price. Corporations found Consumer finance as lucrative as expansion by internal financing. They turned outward for their investment funds, and concentrated on Consumer finance. The Economy boomed. Households began to re-enter the middle class, and employment rolls started to grow; producing added Consumer Demand.

Business leadership remained mis-trained by the Reagan administration. They dreamed of the huge economic profits of the previous age. They started to pressure Congress to change the tax laws, allowing them to again internal finance. The tax burden was again shifted downward, and Consumers once again started to pay for economic profits of Corporations through product price increases. Bush the Younger entered office, and immediately brought back all the tax inequities of the Reagan years. Consumer Demand started to drop immediately, and unemployment started to rise. Consumers began the process of close budgeting once more, with deferments of necessary Consumer products until forced. The Economy is tanking once more, with Supply-Side Economics again showing a losing score.

Another losing proposition appeared with the 1970s in the field of Economics, an ideation which works hard to destroy American economic potential. This is the view of the national debt which states there is no transfer of burden to future generations. This is patently false, which Buchanan showed; though based on the wrong premise. National debt gives the future a list of dedicated resources—the famous 'let Us spend your money for you'. Advocates of the no-transfer view of the National debt say people of the present owe people of the present, not the future. They do not account for the real fact people of the Present only pay interest to people of the Present, letting final payment glide into the future.

Accumulation of National debt has a serious number of consequences for the future generations. It allocates resources of future generations, by establishing a special class of entitlement recipients, formed by their Parents' action of purchase of Treasury Notes. This disturbs the balance of Income distribution for future generations, as well as prolonging a privileged class based on other than economic efforts. It limits the ability of future generations to enter into debt financing for their own benefit. Big Government debt demands Big Government debt service, with prolongation of Big Government activity. It finally stands as a shift of the tax burden forward, with future generations expected to pay for expenditures of today.

The 1950s and 1990s America serve as the highest periods of economic performance ever observed in the history of the World. Future generations may hope to equal the economic performance of these periods, but will be hard pushed to exceed them. The Future faces innumerable problems which the Present Generation refuses to deal with: Increasing population, shrinking resources, the spread of sewage and landfills, the increasing toxification of the Environment, and limited Water resources. The Present Generation claims We cannot maintain lifestyle without the incurrence of more National Debt (We cannot pay Our own bills). So it is decided by Present leadership that the future should pay both Our leftover bills plus their own.

The Author must state he does not believe in a Doomsday scenario. Technology can and will handle every problem which becomes a life-threatening issue for Humanity. He does believe the Population growth will be canceled by a series of plagues. They are the traditional methods of population reduction. Already the field of Medicine suffers from viral and bacterial strains expressing complete immunity to drugs; a situation which will continue to grow. He finds genetic research producing strains of Crops resistant to Herbicides so mass spraying can be utilized; predicting weeds integrating the Gene, will be discovered within a decade. This will nullify all basic Herbicides, and entail a return to normal cultivation; farmers returning to a fate which was always theirs. Technology is a two-edged sword, and We must handle it with care. It will save Humanity though!

Excise taxes function simply as economic profits, which are demanded by Government for tax revenues. They share the exact detriment to economic performance with all other forms of economic profits. Politicians love Excise taxes because they enable Government to tax heavily, below the radar of public awareness. The Public takes notice of these taxes occasionally, but with the absence of Government sharing of information; people assume such taxes cannot be of much moment. Government refusal to issue information comes from fear of public reaction to the list of taxes, and how much revenue derives from those taxes. Excise taxes exceed revenues from Personal Income taxes in the Federal Budget. These taxes reside on top of thousands of product prices without public notification. They are collected from the manufacturer or from the distributor; deliberately collected before the product can even reach the Retailer. Excise taxes are the Soft Money of Government, almost identical to the Soft Money of the Political Parties; hidden from view, hidden in total cost, and the fuel of Congressional Pork Barrel projects.

Few economic studies can be found examining the impact of Excise taxes upon the Economy. It stands as clear these taxes possess more detrimental impact upon Consumer Demand than Personal Income taxes. This is not merely because revenues from Excise taxes exceed the revenues of Personal Income taxation. Extra detrimental effect occurs because of their area of placement, before derivation of Retail expense and profits. The Consumer pays not only the excise tax, but the Retailers' profit on the tax, and the added interest on the Consumer loans. The Author estimates every dollar raised as excise tax, costs Consumer Demand and Consumption about $2.50. This is not the only cost of Excise taxation.

The impact on in-line production of use of Parts under excise taxation must incur all the charges of Production percentage profitability. A combination of a number of such tax placements can easily double the price to distributors, with follow-along profit-taking for the distributor and Retailer. The Consumer can easily find his capacity to consume such products cut to one-third of his original potential.

Environmental protection stands completely outside the Author's proficiency, but failure to put bite into EPA production controls places incredible burden upon the Taxpayer. Environmental clean-up activities have cost at least one-half trillion dollars, and probably more than a trillion dollars. Congressional suppression of EPA power at the behest of Special Interests simply assures such clean-up efforts will be continued long into the future; with escalating costs as the problems mount. Governmental policy is very wrong in this area.

The economics of Technology must be examined at this point, for here lay another failure of proper Government economic intervention. Patent royalties must be set specifically based on the percentage value to the final product, not negotiated by privates parties; bringing restriction from utilization. A Technology Board should be organized by Government, like the Federal Reserve, which sells the technology for the Patent holder; just like the Federal Reserve advances capital for investment or consumption. This throws the advantages of technological advance open to all, with only a consistent, rational payment to the Patent holder. Economies of scale for an entire range of patented products could reduce Costs by fifty percent, especially in the Drug industry. The Patenting entity would still receive a realistic value for the patent, without constricting productivity. We must renovate current practice, if We are to develop the standard of living We all desire.

We have long-term issues with production, because of down-the-road health care concerns. We need a Safety Board, which would decide if a product line is beneficial; through a balance of benefits and risks. The FDA does this now, very poorly, but We need a Board which makes these decisions throughout the economy. This would be a major Government agency, and an regrettable expansion of Government; but it must be organized. Business could be induced to abide by this agency, if Product Producers were paid for the delay of production, and if foreign products were also precluded from Sale in American markets, until Product approval was obtained. A relevant methodology would be a twelve month delay of Patent issuance, until Safety Board approval was obtained.

National Energy policy remains a disgrace, especially since the arrival of the Bush administration. Industry leadership has been allowed complete independence from regulation, without even reportage of import statistics being advanced. Utility rates are basically set by the Providers without oversight. The entrance of Bush the Younger brought an end to any development of alternative energy sources, even those of high effective reliability. A lack of true Energy policy has emerged glaringly.

Importation of energy sources should be placed under Congressional Committee with quota limits set, which can only be raised by Congressional action. All Energy companies would bid for allotments from the set quota. This would have the very real benefits of Congressional supervision of energy prices, without excise taxes. Congress would buy foreign fuel at the best prices (even from American companies Overseas), and resell it to domestic distributors. Congress would control the amount of importation, sell it at market bid so as to reflect real cost, and make it's gas revenues from sale of foreign supplies. Federal fuel excise taxation would be removed from the fuel, and retail price for energy would reflect real costs of importation. The Congressional oversight agency developed would possess power to control internal energy prices without regulation, press the development of alternative energy development through price policy, and eliminate Trade deficits by draft of financial resources from the energy companies.

Economic examination of such a control of energy resource importation expresses many positive benefits. Economic profits(both Government-generated and Private) would be eliminated through competition, bidding on the fuel allotments giving advantage to those energy companies operating only on percentage profits of production. The Congressional purchasing agency would hold real place in the International Energy market, able to counteract OPEC, and demand performance pricing in purchasing energy resources. Energy companies would quickly develop alternative sources of energy, faced with a monopoly seller plus a limited supply. Shipping charges would be reduced to rates not incorporating economic profits, as the purchasing agent would be the largest shipper in the World. The American Merchant Marine and American Shipbuilding could be rebuilt, as Congress mandated imported fuel must be carried in American bottoms. Congress could match the Federal Reserve in inflation-deflation control, through mandatory raises in fuel price, to control the draft or release of funds into the Economy.

A graduated fuel tax could be instituted on the personal level. The Author has long advocated Social Security cards issued to imitate current Credit Cards. Such Cards could be used to institute a graduated fuel tax, taxing the Consumer based on the amount of fuel used within a month. A tax of this kind would start at the basic State fuel tax level, and increase by amounts set by average milage per vehicle type (personal car, bus, or truck). Personal cars would be given two hundred miles per month at the base level, with a twenty percent rise in price for every two hundred miles over the last tax rate. Trucks would have a separate rate from personal cars, and remain at the base level through 6,000 miles per month, with a twenty percent raise thereafter (initially the type of vehicle will be inputted by the station cashier, later the nozzles can be adapted to fit only trucks larger than two tons.). Buses would pay only the base rate.

This tax would be an excise tax, admittedly; but it would accurately reflect foreign importation costs of fuel. Federal law should start to restrict energy industry discounts to major consumers of energy, now in place. Current payments do not reflect the true energy cost of industrial products, and place an effective tax on other Consumers in the region; paying for the excess use of major consumers of energy. The One-User rate will force economic profits from these products to maintain market share, and constrict eventual Consumer demand for these products, in favor of more energy-viable products.

The above proposals, including the latter, will generate higher levels of Consumer Demand after readjustments. Government economic policy will be rationalized, with controls of adequate nature to affect the Economy without dominating the Economy. Decentralized decision-making is retained with the marketplace, facing only what are resource costs instituted by the Government. Congressional restriction of economic profits and internal financing will be discussed in the next Chapter.

[Author's Note: The United States must position itself in the International Energy market as a unified buyer; today, prices of barrels of Oil are purchased with variances of price of up to 45%, due to pre-existing contracts, use of preferred suppliers, and market swings. The payment of a Government-set royalty for Patent rights would cut drug prices to Consumers by at least half of the difference between generic and brand-name drugs. It works equally well in other areas. Failure of Environmental controls only means down-the-road increased cleanup costs.]

9

Government Tax Policy

The Government, today, presents the greatest obstacle to economic performance. It is spending at deficit levels, has placed the tax burden on the wrong elements of society, and it's regulations restrict market flows. It's activity mandates a almost Four percent inflation rate, with no added dimensional expansion. Congressional inaction allows Health Care costs to skyrocket, to the point where Social Security deductions replace Income taxes removed on the Working Class Poor. Pork Barrel projects constitute 12–15% of the Federal Budget, with expected rates of growth in excess of ten percent per year since the Reagan administration. Wage costs of Civil Service personnel increase at a faster rate than the program growth they implement. Government purchase contracts are so bloated in price, around 41% above Private average; they themselves likely produce one percent of Inflation per year. Political campaign funds reach such largesse, they must be considered an Industry sector in themselves. Problems mount by the day, while increasing numbers propel legislation insulating them from market forces. The Author hates to sound like Right-wing militia groups, but the Government has become the enemy!

The list of wrongs on the part of the Government will be quite long in this Chapter, because of the Author's belief that taxation comes in many forms, not just from IRS assessments. Every mal-progression of Government provides a hidden tax upon the Economy, as the Private Sector has to pay for Government expenditures. This tax comes in the form of consumed resources, as well as dollars taken from taxpayers' pockets.

One of the greatest costs to Americans resides in Government constructions. Federal Government holdings—excepting National Parks, Reserves, military bases and Reserves—still almost equals State-owned properties of all fifty States—excluding State Parks and schools. This is to house activity which is only one-tenth of the effort produced by the fifty States, with a employed force less than a fifth. The Author estimates the agricultural lands equal of two States of the Midwest could be doubled, if Federal land were redirected to agriculture with all building and pavements removed. This monopoly of economic resources obviously costs the Economy a two or three percent of NDP. The fifty States should demand proof of reasonable use, or return of the property held by the Federal Government.

The Federal Civil Service is an abomination, evolved into an aristocratic class outlawed by the U.S. Constitution. Most would laugh at this designation, considering the level of income of Civil Servants; but here is the exact problem. All Civil Servants at Federal level draw Middle Class income, whether they are Janitors, Cooks, Secretaries, parking attendants, or waitresses. Private Sector labor would have to pay around $15,000 per year to get equivalent medical care. The minimum firing time for a Federal Civil Servant stands at around 36 months, before all appeals are exhausted; they are paid throughout the Period, though they do not have to show up for work.

They cannot be shifted geographically to work, without their consent; they cannot be ordered to change their occupational designation at all. They can refuse any educational training which extends beyond their occupational designation, and must be allowed training upon request, if it conforms to some area of their occupational designation. Superiors must show cause, and legally-contestable extreme cause, not to advance Civil Servants based upon seniority. Pay scales are based upon seniority and rank; rank totally dependent upon seniority, unless the Civil Servant refuses his advance, which they hold right to do if such advance would alter the nature of their duties. The Federal Civil Servant uniformly receives thirty percent greater pay than their Private Sector counterparts, except in the higher pay grades. Their pensions remain almost 60% higher than their Private Sector counterparts, and they pay only half the portion to those pension funds. They are granted right to retire after a specified number of years, without resort to minimum age requirements like Private Sector counterparts. They automatically gain right to Part-time labor after retirement, if they so desire.

Federal Civil Servant employment once was estimated to cost Private Sector labor around $1.17 per work hour in total tax after all Federal taxes were assessed. The Study was made some time ago, and the Author lost the source; but the cost has probably increased at a rate in excess of the Inflation rate, though the total Federal Civil Service labor force has declined in ratio to Private Sector employment. This aristocracy of labor force remains and it's privileges grow, to the total loss of position of Private Sector labor income and standard of living.

The incredible complexity of Personal Income Tax papers defies human imagination, and costs Private Sector elements almost as much as State Gas taxes. Individuals cannot fill out their own taxes, as they had thirty years previously, Business continues to pay increasing Accountant fees, or Office labor hours, simply to get tax forms filled correctly. The list of tax credits, exemptions, deductions, and deferrals defies counting. No IRS tax region operates according to common rules of collection, granting or denying benefits capriciously. No Taxpayer or IRS litigation ever ends, as Courts cannot define a common direction of decision to render on Tax cases. Accountants and Lawyers gain, as the system breaks down.

Congress passes legislation which generates Government agency regulation, which never disappears. At least half of all documents in Government repositories are not up to date, or relegated to the History sections of the repositories. This seems like a minor issue, but results in half of all business fines for violations of current regulations. The cost is enormous, and even Internet access to Agency Web pages may bring outdated information, because of infrequent review by Agency personnel; some material can be found to be a decade out of date. Business often finds they employ many labor hours filling out forms which are unacceptable; belatedly notified of updated forms. Government does not keep Business in the Loop.

Government inactivity remains a huge cost for Business, as Government agents require up to months to okay paperwork, which a Business manager filled out in five minutes. Business resources set idle while the Government decision-making process runs it's course. A classic example resides in the case of a Developer filing a permission to build a facility from the EPA. This Developer then preceded to enter into negotiations to purchase the land, take Contract bids for Construction, negotiate for a construction contract, get Local zoning permission, and negotiate a Contract for the transport of building materials; finally waiting fourteen months for EPA approval. A worse example is a Manufacturer who was told by OSASHA of a production violation. The Manufacturer asked for a ruling on what further safety precautions needed to be taken. He continued manufacture waiting for a reply, and the Agency filed Court suit against the Manufacturer. The Court ordered the Manufacturer to pay a fine per day of production, backdated to the initial Agency complaint, even though the Government still had not advanced the ruling of proper safety procedures. The snafu goes on.

The sheer volume of regulation negates effective Government action. Congress should waive all regulations, until such time Government agents can prove to an Authorization Court in the District of Columbia that the exact regulation is necessary for efficient operation of either Government, Business, or individual Citizens. This approval would require public contest, with industry or Citizen advocates being present to protest unjust imposition. Many would claim this would only increase bureaucracy, but practical circumstances dictate only immediate necessities would reach public forum, while the inane, idiotic, or unenforceable regulation will never be brought forward by

Government. The benefit to the Economy would be an immediate multi-billion dollar gain, with long-term general regulation which does not insist on dozens of reports which are absurd.

Congress must deal with the Health Care costs of the nation. This means alteration of litigation procedure, but necessitates much more. Congress must take over Malpractice Insurance, paid through licensing of both medical facilities and personnel on basis of percentage of income earned in the area. This should actually be the criteria for malpractice in all licensed occupational employment Economic Purists will insist this is invasion of the Private Sector, but malpractice does not consist of personal risk-sharing; it is a matter of social responsibility in maintenance of minimum performance standards. This definition places malpractice squarely in the realm of Government activity.

The litigation procedure in place assures only lawyers gain. Congress must mandate award limitations for all Damage suits. Corrective damage awards should be allowed at full value, but with Court supervision of the magnitude of said charges; limiting excess pricing by a Social Security administration issued blue book. Punitive damage awards must be set as payments made to the Injured for a set number of years, not to exceed forty, and none higher than the average Income of American taxpayers. Lawyers will be barred from any percentage collection on Corrective damages, and will be allowed to draw personal fees from Punitive awards at no greater rate than fifteen percent per year. The cost of Insurance will immediately drop and will not rise; as awards are tied to the average Taxpayer income.

Punitive damage awards will not be allowed between Business entities, only Restitution awards consisting of Corrective damages plus loss of production profit. Business performance, though, should be criminalized; malfeasance of business conduct should be assigned imprisonment sentences, fines, or both. Civil courts should be empowered to sentence malfeasance of business conduct, as the by-product of Civil suit; judging the guilty party or parties(One or the Other, or both litigants), and assigning imprisonment or fines on basis of degree of guilt.

Lawyers should also suffer the same fate for malfeasance of legal conduct; assigned either imprisonment or fine, for wrongful suit without merit. This informs lawyers there must be discernable damage before bringing suit against normal business or individual conduct; which meets social standards of due caution. The number of lawsuits should begin to drop by as much as fifty percent.

The purported practice of 'Sin Taxes' must be stopped, as must Governmental advertisement of discriminatory practice against any business, business product, industry, or Individual conduct. The Law remains a restrictive agent alone; simply punishing individual violations against individuals with punitive judgements. The Government cannot be allowed discretionary judgements, which should be left to the Judicial system alone. The Government has the right to outlaw specific practice, if it can be proven to be injurious to others. It does not have the right to proclaim a practice as legal, but discriminate against such practice; either by taxation, or by slander. Additional enforcement of excess tax burden, simply because of Practitioner utilization of legal products and behavior, is unconstitutional. There are those who say tobacco and alcohol should be taxed, due to the damage done to society. The Author says there should be a door charge on going to church, like a gate charge at athletic events, and on coffee; both assessed because of violations of public peace, or health considerations. Luckily the Constitution forbids any taxation in any of the areas cited.

Most Economists and Business interests would oppose the proposals of this Chapter, on the grounds there would be a huge increase in Government. Actual study of the proposals, though, clearly expresses a reduction in total Government involvement, as regulation is reduced, and Court-arbitrated conduct replaces. Business costs due to Government intervention in the Economy are both reduced and rationalized. Almost all proposals allow for greater identification of cost magnitudes, degree of liability, and simplify methods of payment. Protection for all is increased, as the need for Government intermediaries declines.

[Author Note: The previous was obviously a social advocacy program, leaving the arena of Economics. It's inclusion remains justified because of the reduction of Costs of Production estimated by implementation of the initiatives. Current Government economy policy stands as anti-quated today, as was the Government economy policy was in meeting the Great Depression of the 1930s. Every Proposal expresses direct need existent today, for the furtherance of economic growth. Each ele-ment faces great Opposition from those who maintain their economic class by the inequities of the current practice. Support must come from those who will escape the current economic duress suffered; Business must lobby as effectively for change, as they have previously lobbied for personal gain measures—both mean profit; one simply fair, compared the discrimination existent today.]

10
New Tax System

Tax Policy Economists differ from other Economists only in their inherent belief that Government intervention in the Economy contains effectiveness solely in it's ability to tax. Readers of the previous Chapter may think the Author abandons this belief; he does not. The previous initiatives were all based on taxation of methodology, remuneration, or malfeasance. The taxation were clearly outlined and set with easy enforcement or collection; all being universal in nature. Each and every concern being a matter of law, not regulation; Government judgements being rational and systematic.

Current Government taxation aches for rationalization, a compilation of junk additions or alterations from the original program of revenue receipt. The dispersion of Congressional dispensations from taxation for special interests has become a maze which even the IRS cannot define. The sole reason Government raises any revenue at all, resides in the inability of common citizenry to comprehend all the loopholes. They simply expect they owe a certain amount of tax, and pay it. Corporations hire informed Accountants, and receive rebates for taxes which they never paid. These Accountants remain not totally informed, the Author estimating the average Accountant misses approximately three hundred dollars of exemptions per individual taxpayer, and forty thousand dollars of exemption for every business Return. Accountants, though, are still afflicted by the outdated notion that some tax should be paid.

The greatest detriment to any Tax system comes in the form of differentiation, or specialization for the less-economically oriented. This descent into differentiation brings ever-increasing splintering of groupings, until soon tax law is being written for specific business enterprise. This is not being fallacious, dozens of tax provisions have been written, which could only impact one to two businesses in a specific industry; IRS representatives specifically required to do Congressional enactment research to find the claimed exemption.

One specialized tax provision allowed for a per person tax exemption per viewer determined by art museum ticket sales, if the viewer viewed specific art paid by the National Endowment for the Arts. The tax exemption was not limited per museum attendance, but by exhibit; one museum gaining 7.5 times the exemption, as the cost of the ticket into the museum. Ninety-nine percent of the museums in the Country never heard of the tax provision, and most of the rest are non-profit organizations not subject to tax. A guess suggests no more than three museums could use this tax provision, and probably only one knew of it. It remains clear simplicity and universality could provide benefit to the tax system.

The place to start must be the top, i.e., the Income Tax system. A simplified Income Tax should be implemented, which applies to all. It should absorb the Corporate Income Tax, the Capital Gains Tax, Personal Income Tax, current Excise Taxes, and Royalties and Rents Taxes. All should be treated equally as Income. Personal exemptions for the taxpayers will be included, with exemption for each dependent. Business will receive a personal exemption per each employee, if said exemption is extended to pay for medical and retirement benefits. The personal exemption will be of one set size for all. There should be no other exemptions, tax credits, or deductions; other than variable business performance or employment expense. Debt servicing exemption from taxation will not exceed twenty percent of before-tax Income. Business will face a Recapitalization Sur-tax, if business cannot prove a certain level of recapitalization expense determined by the IRS as standard for the industry; the Sur-tax being the difference between what was spent, and the standard estimated amount. Business must maintain the viability of the business structure, or be taxed for not doing so. A Research and Development tax credit for business organizations of ten percent will be granted, if the business can prove the expenditure, and the Technology Board or Agency approves the line of development. The basic structure of taxation has been outlined.

Interjection of a Sur-tax of twenty percent on undistributed Profits of Corporations will allow such organizations to maintain operating fund balances without outside financing, but will tax internal financing of expansion. Stockholders will return to Dividend rates consistent with the risk taken for uninsured investments; the Author expects an Eight percent return on normal profit industries. The Stock Market will be supported, not by speculation, but by normal ratios of expected profitability. This could be extended by tax stipulation Stock Options cannot be in excess of Employee salary, without being considered as Corporate profit. Lengthening the process to state any total remuneration of Employees greater than twenty times the Mean remuneration of total Company employees, will be considered as Corporate profits. This remuneration will specifically apply to medical or retirement benefits, paid Insurance, Stock Options, Individual loans, and purchase of Personal property. Declaration of Corporate income simplifies, without distraction of claimed labor payments; with correct channelization of Profits to rightful recipients. Business formation will prosper, as illicit behavior of Corporate leadership is minimized; the environment benefits as Corporate leadership practices normal allocations for infrastructure costing.

Consequences of the proposed tax system can be analyzed. Business is paid to do Research and Development, but they are forced to turn to outside financing for new product-line development. Business must maintain their enterprise viability, or be taxed. Business must provide medical and retirement benefits for their employees, or lose a like amount as tax. Insurance premiums will drop, if the provisions of the foregoing Chapter are implemented; so retirement benefits will increase for Employees over the extended period. Engagement in down-sizing means a reduction of exemptions for the business, and pressure will be removed; profit-taking will be lost to taxation. Layoffs will entail loss of exemptions by quarter, increasing the permanent overhead of business through taxation; employees will be transferred to household duties, or alternative efforts, slowing the speed and duration of layoffs. Business costs will come to reflect true labor costs, and Employees will gain greater security of employment; while Government social expenditures for unemployment benefits and welfare will decline.

The effect on Incomes need clarification. The taxation on undistributed Corporate profits will raise Stockholders' Incomes by about forty percent of the total at the minimum. This will equate to approximately a ten percent rise in their Consumption. The discrimination of the Government against internal financing by Corporations will lead to a seventy percent decline in economic profits pricing, so there should be at least a Six percent decrease in current product prices, over an estimated three year period. Estimated Corporate profits transfer to Employee wages should bring overall Employee Incomes an increase of almost twelve percent. This increase, combined with the estimated product price decline, should produce a minimum increase in Consumer Demand of fifteen percent. The Corporate transfer to external financing should raise loan rates to approximately Six percent, increasing Depositor Incomes up by at least fifty percent, with a twenty percent increase in their Consumption. The Corporate cost of finance should not increase by more than a percent, due to more careful distribution of funds, and a higher profit ratio to investment. The overall impact of the new taxation indicates there would be increased Consumer Demand with reduced product pricing, higher employment, higher benefits to that employment, with greater profitability deriving from that employment and the capital utilized.

Another important change which need be made consists of the method of financing Education in this Country. The process of taxing residential households through property taxes for this Education destroys household consumption patterns, lowers the provision levels of Community services, distorts levels of Educational funding across regional districts due to lack of economic development, and impacts the quality of Student instructional care. National testing expresses quality training levels may vary by as much as forty-seven percent of total knowledge integration. More effective educational funding must be established.

The Social demand for Education is preparation for effective participation as labor in the Economy. This clearly outlines the major beneficiaries of Education reduce to Employers and Employees. Parents remain concerned because they wish their children to succeed in the Economy, but their participation isolates no reward; even less those property holders, whose children are already raised or never were. All are asked to bear a deep economic burden for which there is not remuneration. This economic burden also incites reductions of Consumption for the property holders in excess of Eight percent per school district average.

It becomes obvious Educational funding would possess economic rationale, if borne by Employer and Employee. The answer would be a Wage-borne tax based upon a set fee per hour worked. Employers would immediately protest such taxation could not assess properly the separate educational levels necessary in the Production process. The Author suggests these protests can be met easily.

The first condition which must be established as a axiom, claims a High School education, or equivalent, stands as the minimum educational level capable of operating in Our current Economy. This is what the Employer will be asked to pay. The burden will not be excessive, far less than provision of medical insurance to Employees and their families; and reform of liability laws as mentioned in the previous Chapter, can likely allow payment of the educational tax and provision of medical insurance, at less cost than currently for only the later. Employers may or may not gain by reduction of property taxes, but gain from better provision of Community services. All indications express Employee Consumer Demand would likely increase due to the reduction of property taxes, but even without such reductions; the Educational tax should not affect current Wage levels.

The Employees will be asked to participate in the Educational funding process, on the personal level of paying for advanced training. This can be done by alteration of the Social Security administration Charter. A separate program would be set up for the payment of tuition costs of enrollees in the Social Security system. This would initially be funded either by dispersion from general Federal revenues, or loans made by the Federal Reserve to the Social Security Fund. Employees would repay the refunding of tuition payments, book and housing payments for advanced education, and a nominal weekly stipend; by weekly Social Security deductions from payment in excess of the normal withdrawals, until the total repayment is made. The repayment schedule should be set up over a payment period of twenty years, so Employee Consumer Demand is not seriously affected.

Examination of the total package for Education brings to light many benefits. Employers find themselves paying actually less of an educational cost per labor hour, than they would otherwise; having reduced minimum training standards in hiring practice; allowable with knowledge that the skill levels are attainable. Employees find ability to educate themselves for more lucrative employment, constrained only by understandable set charges of duration. Property taxes can be reserved for provision of Community services, with higher employment levels cheaper than maintenance of the educational establishment. Consumer Demand and Consumption of property holders increase without loss of Community viability, and property maintenance schedules can be easier funded. Local costs will be shared throughout the Economy.

The role of the Social Security administration will be greatly expanded, but in a rational manner; entailing no more than the addition of accounting procedures, and the employment of trained labor to sign up Students. The Social Security Fund already exists as a modified Insurance Fund, and the problems of dispersal and collection can be easily solved; actuary tables indicating levels of repayment loss, with ability to raise overall payments to cover such losses. Educational institutions would be assured of levels of income, with Government ability to limit excessive inflation in Education by limiting total amounts of tuition paid at universal one price for all; dependant on level of educational institution. States would still be mandated with supplying the physical plant for educational purposes; but gaining from advanced levels of skilled labor. The expansion of Government can be limited, and it's impact minimized by universal application, where all would complain about excessive regulation.

The next element must be a special tax on business income to minimize adverse economic initiatives in American society. This Tax measure would simply declare State and Local property taxes as deductions. Non-payment of property taxes to State and Local governments will incite an averaged payment to the IRS; this averaged payment the average of property taxes throughout the United States. This tax negates State and Local governments' discrimination against their own citizens, in order to attract business to the area. The current practice discriminates against older businesses already established, places too high a burden on residential property holders, and leads to excessive infrastructure costs which are not borne by the Users. It also distorts the distribution of economic activity between regions, causing induced levels of unemployment, higher welfare costs for abandoned Communities, and magnified infrastructure and policing costs for Free-Trade zones. This Tax would stop the practice of competitive bidding between regions, and induce local Capital to invest in local area improvement.

The growth of State and Local Sales taxes threaten current Consumer Demand ratios, and will impact any return to growth conditions. Introduced to limit the growth of property taxes and State

Income taxes, today; they are used to fund local Government expansion and rapid increases in Government salaries. All of the above are incredibly expensive to the Private Sector, through both payment and increased Wage demands. The United States has the right by the Constitution to regulate commerce. Congress needs to pass legislation stipulating any Product sold interstate must have no more than a Six percent Sales tax assigned, anywhere it is sold. The Author would stipulate a rate of Two percent, but it would impel a massive downsizing of local governments; with increased area unemployment in areas already suffering. The Law would simply state there could be no further incursion into Consumption levels.

The entire area of Government regulation of business must be altered to reflect business methods of inducement. Congress must pass a specific system of Sur-tax increases on Income, rather than the assessment of fines. This system of Sur-tax increases should be set based upon the amount of damage from violation of regulations, should be automatically imposed by notification of the supervising agency, with business interest allowed to petition the Courts for excessive imposition of Sur-taxes by the agency. The Sur-tax levels will be permanent, until all damage or corrections have been completed. Agency notification to the IRS will begin Sur-tax withdrawals, altering the current practice; where Fines do not have to be paid, until the last Court petition has been exercised. The Courts must impose the least level of Sur-tax, unless business interests can prove the damage has been corrected, or the corrections made. The Courts cannot reverse the decision of the regulating Agency, unless it can be proven to be false in allegation. Violators must pay, unless they can prove they were not in violation; the burden of proof on the Violator.

The minimum level of Sur-tax should be set at Eight percent of total business income after allowable expenses. This is equivalent to the basic Interest charges of external financing to correct the problem. Three additional levels should be present, each level adding Eight percent; until there is a total maximum Sur-tax of 32%. The base level will inform the offending business it is cheaper to correct the offending damage, than pay double for the capital to clean up or correct the damage. The further imposed levels demonstrate resistance will be penalized by regulating Agency by increased level, which will take Court action to reduce. Business learns it is cheaper to comply with social demands, than it is to defy those demands.

The final proposed legislation would be a specific Tax deduction allowed to business, if they can produce product; which will maximize economic resources. This tax deduction will not exceed Five percent of total Profits. It stipulates any manufacturers producing product which has a life-span longer than the average life-span of the product, will receive this tax deduction. This will be determined by the actual history of use of their products of production, over the previous twenty years. This may not seem a worthwhile deduction to Readers, but it cancels current policy of limited life-span of product to maintain Sales; and will lead to long-term usage of better construction methods.

The major component necessary for any tax system must be universality of application. A common Income Tax which does not discriminate between Individual, Capital Gains earner, Business, or Landlord will reduce tax rates to the lowest levels capable of paying the expenses of Government. All are One in insistent demand for the lowest rates. All are taxed based upon their participation in the Economy, not in political activities. Government and Court no longer threaten the economic viability of Anyone, on any level. Social demands are met, without Government intrusion into normal market forces. Government impediment to economic growth are removed, replaced with Adam Smith's 'invisible hand' of market determination.

[Author's Note: The above Chapter may seem complex to some, but the limited number of universal applications could be written in a twenty-page Tax Act; compared with some number of pages last heard to be in excess of 1500. The best method of amplifying the above provisions is to discuss their most likely effects. Each Income Tax level would probably enjoy a percentage drop of taxation, as increased revenues came from elimination of multiplicity of tax credits. Business would be paid to recapitalize, in the avoidance of taxation for failure to recapitalize. Labor demands will find less opposition from Management, as it cannot retain undistributed taxes without taxation. Almost all Employees would be granted medical and retirement benefits. Stockholders would get increased dividends, while Business profits would actually go up from better-regulated production; even faced with the cost of debt service from external financing. Research and Development would be funded, as it is given a tax credit. Consumer Product prices will go down, or not increase; as economic profits are removed from the pricing mechanism.]

11
Government Expenditures.

Multitudes of Economic studies have examined the impact of the Government on the Economy. Hardly a section of Government activity fails of acute examination of economic effects. The wealth of material concerning Income-transfer payments made by Government cost more in terms of labor hours of compilation along with paper and printing expenditures, than an average California County expenditure in such payments. There remains a sincere study of economic theory of Government's role in the Economy.

The most simplistic economic theory of Government states Government is identical to a business inside the market, simply a supplier of a product called Infrastructure. Taxpayers emulate Buyers in the general market, buying elements of infrastructure at the cheapest possible price. Government sells it's product for what the market will bear, i.e., the taxes they can impose; not counting the debt load Government may assume, a form of cheating to this simplistic model. Taxpayers theocratically control the mix of infrastructure they purchase, by denial of taxes or changing the management of the Government. The Author has personal affection for this Model which ignores reality; but has a directness that entertains.

The next, more complex Model insists Government is the most powerful industry in the Economy. Government purchase expresses the Consumer Demand of the totality of the population, as opposed to only partial Consumer Demand of the other participants in the market. This Model claims the total Consumer Demand raises capital for purchase through taxation and debt acquisition. This Consumption fulfills the common desires of the people in the Economy, and reduces the Consumption of other elements in the Economy. This Model again suffers from delusion (separation from reality), not identifying the methodologies of tax legislation; or the procedure of Government dispersions.

A third Model views Government as basically Consumer in the Economy. It purchases it's needs from the Private Sector, taxing other Consumers to raise the revenues; government debt ascribed as future tax impositions. Government supplies infrastructure to other Consumers in the Economy, who desire maximization of the benefits of their own personal Consumption. The Government, under this Model, must be induced to purchase like any Consumer; hence the need for advertising campaigns portraying the advantages of Consumption through political activity. Government is seen as the vehicle to maintain full production, through added increments of advertising.

A more discouraged Model finds Government to be an oppressive tyrant in the Economy, agent of Income-transfers; distorting and destroying natural market allocations, to implant an artificial distribution of goods and services. This Model perceives any Government expenditure above direct purchase of hard product for national defense or infrastructure as curtailment of market expansion; the summation dictated by the interplay of Supply and Demand. The Model detailed Government employment costs as unnatural drafts from the Economy, reducing skilled labor at the expense of excess Wage costs to the Private Sector, and considering such payments a loss of Profit to both Business and Labor. Income-transfers block proper incentive for both Labor and Business, and increases of Consumer Demand from these activities considered to be a direct loss of Investment capital.

A more sophisticated Model suggests Government remains the regulator of economic performance, supplying economic incentive by it's creating Consumer Demand by Income-transfers and employment of labor. This views holds Government should spend more under recessive conditions, hiring more employees, and giving out support payments. The primary thesis being Government can turn the Economy from Recession to Growth, by the expenditure of debt-raised revenues. They insist Government debt is not debt, but simply redistribution of revenues over time. The Model insists the Government should run a debt for peak economic performance, financing debt only when the Economy is overheating and creating Inflation.

Another Model contests the expansion of Government debt, asserting the debt curtails financial reserves and consumes resources at a rate to be the cause of Inflation. Payment of Government debt release financial reserves, and this repayment should be scheduled to suppress inflation. Capital investment should be maximized, with the extension of Consumer credit to assure profitability for the capital investment schedule. This Model translates to a statement Consumers should bear the debt, not Government; though certain levels of Government debt are mandatory for Inflation suppression. The Model coincides with the next Model, both proclaiming Business taxation should be low or nonexistent.

This Model determines economic advantage to Government participation in the Economy only comes through Government provision for business needs. Business taxation should be non-existent with the costs of Government borne entirely by Consumers uninvolved in the capital aggregation function. Excise taxes plus Personal Income taxes separated from Capital Gains or Business taxation should be suppliers of Government revenues. Government debt must be acquired only for the purpose of Government supply of lucrative purchasing contracts to Private Business. Sharp limitation of this Debt should be in place, because of it's drain on financial resources for capital investment. Welfare payments should be discontinued, so that increased labor reserves would lower Wage Costs to Business; and reduce living expense for Labor for the same reason. The Model hates Income redistribution, unless it is to Business.

The above Models all share one failing: They ignore the humanism of the Economy. Their correlations always falter under stress, this stress consistently generated by the human strata of the Economy. Economic growth demands full human participation in the Economy; this does not mean Everyone must work or produce. It defines the necessity for all Participants to act in the manner required for good economic performance. The best way might be by examples.

The Author knows of a Handyman, who has a place to stay, and who makes fifty to sixty dollars per week. He is happy and content, hates regular employment, and stay warm and fed by charity and odd jobs. He cannot be counted as a Consumer, but he is a valuable element of the Economy; serving the basic needs of his odd job employers. Most, especially Economists, would criticize this Individual, because he is not a productive element of the Economy. The fact of the matter remains that he is, and overall economic performance suffers from the lack of these Individuals when they are absent.

The Author also know another Individual, who makes around six thousand dollars per week. The Individual also does not work, collecting earnings from a family inheritance. Economists would stipulate this Individual is a productive member of the economic family, because of his receipt of the six thousand per week. These funds have to be spent or re-invested, so the Individual is a participating element in the Economy. The Individual does indeed spent only $300 per week, thinking Society is out to rob him of his wealth through low interest and dividend rates of return. He does re-invest the rest of the income.

A third Individual of the Author's experience works very hard, and has a substantial income from this labor. Economists love this Individual because he is both laborer and Consumer. They would attest this is the proper format and lifestyle for all elements in the Economy. The Individual remains not perfect: he has a lazy, profligate wife who uses her control of the Individual to evade labor, and spend excessive amounts. The Individual also has a number of children in college, and who resemble their mother more than their father. The Individual discusses the possibilities of taking bankruptcy with the Author, though he has an Income to rival the above-described Miser.

The final example will be an Individual who works, but not well; and makes less than twenty thousand per year. All Economists would declare this Individual to be a productive element of the economy, though most would criticize the inferior productivity of his employment. An Author stipulation stating the Individual uses Credit Cards in excess, and has over eighty thousand dollars worth of debt; cancels his value for most Economists, for he is a certain for bankruptcy. The loss of the Credit capital extended, expresses the fact the Individual is a liability to economic performance.

Examination of the four examples tells of mal-performance within the Economy. The first individual actually provides more production to the Economy than he receives in services or goods from the Economy. The second Individual does not Consume to the level expected of his Income level, and does not actually provide supervision to entrepreneurial investment, so provides no economic value at all. The third Individual provides full measure of production to economic performance, but allows parasitic considerations to Consume more than his level of production. The last Individual provides the minimum level of economic production, to garner abeyance of critique of his excessive Consumption. All four examples provide expression for economic malpractice.

Economists ignore the humanism in the Economy to their peril, and defeat of all projections which do not account for human reactions. This humanism produces the reactions to economic incentives operating in the economy. The first example undervalued his labor, thereby losing his ability to consume and his ability to save. The second undervalued his Consumption, because of perceived value of remuneration. The third fully understood his value to production, but allowed personal ties to press his Consumption above his production. The fourth felt his employment was undervalued in terms of his desire to consume. None of the above would be worthy of note, except it is exactly misplacement of economic incentives which cause losses of economic performance.

Undervaluation of Labor brings on the first and fourth cases, in the first case by disinclination for regular employment, in the second case a refusal to retard Consumption levels to match productivity payments. Undervaluation of capital returns causes the second example to retard his Consumption, to make up for shortfalls in expected returns on capital investment. Excessive ease of Credit allows both the third and fourth examples to maintain Consumption levels unsustained by productivity. All cases express error in placement of economic incentive values.

Excessive ease of Credit can be proven to sharply reduce the value of Wages; proven by mathematical models which the Author would find hard to duplicate. Every dollar of Consumer credit at interest rates less than 4.1% (actual Consumer credit card rates less than 12%) causes 1.57 dollars loss of purchasing power from all hourly Wage scales less than $12.45 per hour. Every dollar of Business credit extended below 6.1 percent, causes $.74 loss of purchasing power for all Wages and salaries less than $63,000 per year. Ease of Credit can be a regressive taxation upon labor, and is accumulative through the life-span of products produced and sold by this eased Credit. Actual labor becomes increasingly unattractive in the face of extended ease of Credit.

Relaxation of Inheritance taxation creates a Parasite class, who neither productively performs, or exercises personal supervision of investments. This class has neither earned the wealth, or manages it. Their Consumption pattern stands thirty percent higher for each and every Income class above $50,000 per year, than the same Income levels who perform in the Economy. This differential alone increased the Consumption cost of the same number of Individuals as the numbers in the parasite class, but are in Income classes below $30,000 per year; by almost two percent per year, due to consumption of resources. This parasitic class can be expected to increase by about 12% per generation under the current Inheritance tax rates, and rise to over forty percent per generation if Inheritance taxes are removed. Removal of Inheritance taxes could mean a thirty percent increase in Consumption Costs per year for Income levels of less than $30,000 per year, within twenty years. The addition of wage increases to these working classes will not mean an increase in purchasing power, only Inflation; as the consumption rate of the expanded parasite class will still consume the resources.

Economists would insist this class would consume like resources, whether they inherit or not. The fact remains their entrance into the labor market would reduce Wages, but increase purchasing power of Wage-earners. This entrance would bring a like increase in production levels, and propel technology through profit from Sales to develop alternative resources. The above-mentioned reduction of Wages could not exceed the current rate of purchasing loss due to this class. It must be remembered Economists talk of reduced Wages, when speaking of a reduced rate of Wage increase; Wages not expected to actually reduce in dollar amounts. A parasitic class forced to labor could not consume at the above-average rates currently expressed, and production increases would minimize Price increases. Reduction of the numeral magnitude of this parasite class must be conducted, else face increased distortions in Wage rates.

The impact of Inheritance taxes also suffers an innate distortion. Inheritance receives treatment as earned income of the estate, which it is not. This places the Deceased as the responsible party for payment of taxation. Probate courts suffer incredible delays as relayed assets, yet unsettled, earn income from which tax must be paid; and all debts and disbursements owed before death must be paid, before heirs can be paid. Years may pass before Tax returns can be discontinued for the dead Individual; the Author had a grandparent still filing Capital Gains reports twelve years after death, because of defrayed Will conditions of lifetime occupancy of property for his wife. A debasing debacle for all!

Probate courts should impound all assets for the Government, pay all debts and defrayed disbursements, and turn all funds over to a Federal Inheritance Reserve. Inheritance should be passed to the heirs as personal income, subject to tax as Personal Income, and limited in total amount of receipt. Family businesses can be maintained by sale from the Federal Inheritance Reserve of such businesses to heirs, at consistent loan rates for commercial properties. The Federal Inheritance Reserve would be responsible for all debts of the Deceased, paid through the Probate courts. Discussion of the allowable Inheritance allotment for heirs should allow for comfortable lifestyle for the heirs, but no economic control of market forces. The Author like the image of three million dollars. Lesser inheritances would be charged only Personal Income tax on the inheritance, while all funds over the allotments would revert to the general Treasury; as would interest and principal from sale of commercial properties by heirs or Government Treasury agents.

An interesting formulation of the above Plan for Inheritance becomes the right of the Deceased to name as many heirs as desired, prior to death. This provides for a Wealth redistribution which even Conservatives would find hard to oppose. Wealthy Individuals would be inclined to dispense heirs in huge numbers by favoritism, rather than let their wealth revert to the Treasury. This process would permit the economic gains made by the Individual, to be spread socially; for the increase in living standards for all of Society. Impact on charities would be minimal, as such funds would be diverted from limited heirs as is current practice. Commercial properties under such an Inheritance Plan, would bear the same capital return burden as is common among regular business operation; this insisting there would be no economic profits from 'free capital' endowments. Therefore, tight managerial supervision will be required; eliminating the detachment of supervision from ownership. Such an Inheritance Plan could in consequence add a potential two or three percent of total economic value per year to an averaged forty billion dollars a year of death reallocation.

There currently exists a great animosity among Economists for what can be called Welfare payments, whether Private Sector or Government. These payments include medial and life insurance, disability payments, liability settlements, and retirement payments. Supply-Side Economists claim these charges distract from economic performance, and business should be free of such provision. Economic reality in a modern Economy declares such welfare payments must be possessed by labor, in order for labor to function; not just as productive elements, but in their role as Consumer. The lack of such provision cuts their productivity drastically, and retards their Consumption by as much as thirty percent. These benefits can be provided by labor-acquired insurance, Government program, or business-acquired insurance.

Study of Insurance programs indicate labor-acquired insurance on a personal basis costs approximately 23–37% more than group insurance packages acquired by business. Government program supply of these welfare payments expresses benefit packages about twenty percent higher than private insurance, and claim-adjustment costs approximately three times the operating costs of private insurance. Normal distribution of taxation shows business pays $1.34 for Government supply of these welfare payments, as compared to $1 of benefit paid by private Insurer in group insurance plans. The personal supply by Labor of personal insurance requires around a 17% increase of Wages, over such supply by group insurance. It can also be shown 62% of such payments can be claimed through sympathetic Courts under Liability insurance, insuring business has to pay such Costs as Liability insurance premiums.

Study of the profusion of avenues of Claim details business has to pay at least seventy percent of all such welfare payments under current practice, and business group insurance provision of such payments could save business 14% of the total cost. The added burden of group insurance cannot be greater than 16% of the total value of such dispersals, with reduced Wage demands under the provision of group insurance. Liability insurance premiums could reduce as much as fifty percent with Tort reform, and transfer of liability to group insurance programs. This further reduces the cost to business of welfare payments to labor.

Economic models must reflect the humanism of the Economy. Participants in the economy will not react with the vigor for economic performance, if they are not properly provisioned with economic incentives. This process does not merely mean reductions in production, but also the more important arena of Consumption. There cannot be profits without Consumption. Consumer demand becomes the God of all Economists, because Consumer Demand dictates sixty percent of the Consumption of any Economy. The necessities of Consumption, and the Profits to be made from it, will be considered in the next Chapter.

[Author's Note: The Author has real aversion to the generational transfer of economic wealth. It is his belief that the transfer of wealth to Individuals who have not endured the economic labor of deriving it's gain, leaves a loose cannon with an Idiot at the trigger. He once proposed an Inheritance program where the Government took and sold it all, and heirs were simply guaranteed a yearly stipend based upon the Principal, but not the interest on the Principle; for as long as the Principal lasted, payments automatically dispersed at levels allowing for forty years' payment. He deemed it fair payment, if there was a limit placed on magnitude of any given monthly payment of $3000; and almost got into a physical fight with an Individual destined to receive a Twelve million dollar inheritance.]

12

Consumption

Consumption stands as the end-process of the Economy, like unto Death being the end of life. It contains the destruction of the production achieved in the Economy, but programmed destruction which improves the human condition in it's loss. Consumption, itself, provides resource for future production, as does Death for life. Resources are recovered, certainly; though the real renewal comes in the profits from the sale of products for Consumption. Profits of this Consumption, in loosest terms, may be the considered the fertilizer for future growth.

Consumption, though, differs from Death in the fact it must be paid for. Payment for this Consumption comes in a set number of ways: Sale of resources, Wages, Sale of past Wages (royalties), Rent of resources or capital, and Profits from previous consumption. Study of these methods declare there is only one given, resources, and all others have to be earned. Further contemplation states resources are themselves a product of work; having required the prerequisite efforts to stake out and claim the resources. Financial capital is only the accumulated earnings from Wages, Royalties, Rents, or Profits which have not been spent in consumption. Rents insist only claim of the Property and investment in the property; both the product of labor or financial capital. Profits come from performing the effort of production. All amount to nothing more than different forms of Wages.

All forms of financial remuneration remain Wages, differing only in the method of payment. Consumption remains driven by Wages alone, though the methods of payment produce different forces upon the Economy; altering the nature of production. Financial capital finds creation through deferment of Consumption in funds collected by one of the methods of payment of Wages. Most Economists would insist financial capital is thereby limited, because of the limitation of Wages; all due to the number of laborers along with their rates of unconsumed Wages. This is not the reality!

The entrance of Debt produces a draft against future Wage payments in whatever form. This borrowing from future earnings is limited not by the labor force, but only by the expected largesse of future Wage payments. Expression of this criteria says One can borrow to build an economic productive unit of assured repayment of the borrowed Wages, plus a greater expected return; One can borrow against this greater expected return to build more economic productive units. There only has to be surety of future earnings for these economic productive units.

Two things provide the needed surety of future earnings: recoverable resources units, and a Consumption market to purchase the products from which the earnings are supposed to derive. Recoverable resource units are always limited by the presence of raw material, the technology for extracting this raw material, the amount of labor units present to extract this raw material, the amount of capital equipment existent to extract this raw material, and demand for these resources produced by conflicting uses for these resources. Consumer demand for these resources establish the price for these resources, pay for the capital equipment and labor assets to extract them, pay for the research to develop the technology, pay the Rents necessary for resource material extraction; and determine the amounts of resources available, through the profitability existent from extracting the material resource.

Clearly evident is the constriction resource pricing places upon future expected earnings, but the limitation of resource supply also constricts future expected earnings; both the product of Consumer demand. Final Consumption also constricts future expected earnings, through reduced demand for the products produced as the price of the products rise. Future expected earnings are canceled by limited resource, excessive resource pricing, reduced consumption from excessive product price, or loss of Profits from reduced product pricing to induce consumption. In every case the expansion of financial capital is limited solely by future expected earnings, which are limited by Consumer demand for Consumption.

Economic studies produce statistical readouts which validate the statements of the Author. Rises of resource pricing, reduction of resource supply, rise of product pricing, and lowering of Consumer demand for either resources or final product; actually does lower the provision of financial capital, in studies analyzing debt ratios and pricing. Government expenditures actually increase resource pricing, and thereby restricts the provision of financial capital. Lay people may not understand the ramifications of this conceptualism, but economic studies completely nullify the assertions of Keynesianism, Monetarism, and Tri-plane Economics. All economic fuel provided to an Economy must be based upon increasing Consumer Demand.

Simple Keynesianism simply increases Government spending with increases in resources pricing at evaluated ratios. Monetarism proposes expansion of Consumer credit, but without limitation of resource and product pricing, so such expansion only propels inflation without growth. Tri-plane Economics vastly increases resources prices, through production ratios scaled to produce without profit through excessive levels of production; while vastly constricting Consumer demand in the market expected to pay for the capitalization of production. The total produces inflation at reduced production levels. Supply-Side Economics ignore Consumer demand, ease capitalization of production, evade the Costs of production to insure lower Wage payments, and project production schedules which could only be fulfilled by unending Consumer Demand. The most business-oriented Economists, Supply-Siders cannot understand how they produce a resource price-driven Inflation, produce the lowest Profits from production, destabilize financial institutions, and record the highest levels of bank and business failures.

Economists demand advance of alternative economic policy, before dismissal of current policy; correctly emphasizing the need for coherence in economic policy. The rest of the Chapter will attempt to present a flexible policy with possible means of deviation, to counteract generated adverse economic conditions; which are outside the normal function market conditions.

The first statement must be the preservation of Consumer Demand remains the key to economic performance, due to the fact it stands as the sole drive of Consumption; this the only motivation and drive of production. Economic production and growth cannot be maintained without sufficient Consumer Demand. Initiatives must operate to increase discretionary spending potential of Consumers, without providing fuel to Inflation in either resource or product markets. Financial capital growth is actually a direct function of the growth of Consumer Demand, and can actually expand with the rise of interest rates. Close supervision of resource markets conducted so levels of resource supplies expand, without price increases. The total can only be kept within balance with limitations of Government spending.

The Start position comes with amendment of the tax laws, so tax burden spreads equally among all Income classes; this is not proposal of a One-Rate tax. All Income earners should be taxed, but the Poor should be limited only to Social Security deductions. Increase of tax burden should be increased according to additions to discretionary income levels: discretionary income additions estimated by total Income minus the debt load of the Income level as a whole. This level of discretionary income should be averaged per Taxpayer, then multiplied by twelve percent for each $10,000 above the base of $20000. The base level of Income taxation above $10,000 but below $20,000 would be taxed ten percent. At no time is the Income tax to exceed

44% of total Individual income at any level. This level is set for the specific necessity of continued viability of financial institutions to organize financial capital.

Business and Employees will be mandated to underwrite Education by payroll taxes, which pay for lower education by hourly rates; and higher education on personal level of use by Employees. Business are to be given tax deductions based on labor roll levels alone; none to be given unless proven to be devoted to medical, disability, and retirement benefits for Employees. Studies have shown curtailment of Government welfare payments reduce Recipient Consumer Demand rates much faster than integration into the labor market raises personal Consumer demand; an estimated forty-three percent never regaining previous Consumer demand rates. This expresses physical infirmities and mental ineptitude of Recipients limit entrance in the labor market; resulting in no marked depression of Wage rates. Pressure should be removed from the issuance of welfare payments, with added incentives given to retraining procedures for these Recipients.

The easing of pressure from such welfare payments should include supervision from Civil Service personnel. Such supervision costs almost seventy times what it recovers in welfare fraud prevention, with only a twelve percent reduction in such welfare frauds. Civil Service personnel possess a Work Skills ratio of transfer to the Private Sector labor market without loss of income of over 81%; compared to the transfer ratio of Welfare recipients of less than forty percent without loss of income, such intense supervision is uneconomical.

Government reduction of expenditures must come in areas where Consumer Demand is not reduced. Government supply contracts can be limited to no greater profitability for Suppliers, than exceeded by similar contracts by Private Sector industry. Cost Overruns can only include added labor charges and supply costs, specifically prohibited by law to include Profits from the Cost Overruns; management and stockholder acceptant their participation profits only extend to the initial contract.

All distinct programs of the Federal Government must accept the canopy of some Federal Department, including Congressional aides and Assistants who will fall under Justice Department supervision. The only exception will be the Federal Reserve system, which will maintain independence. All budgets for all such programs will be allocated from the general Department budget it is assigned to, said budget funds allocated from the general budget of the Federal department by department leadership. The governing Department will have overview of all budget applications, and integrate such budget funds into their overall budget.

Financial institutions must be regulated for the purpose of effecting proper rates of return on deposit accounts. There has been increasing efforts by both Government and financial institution to limit those returns, which adversely affect capital aggregation by these institutions. The Author proposes federal legislation banning any financial charges for provision of financial services by financial institutions; simply demanding financial institutions gain all profitability from their loan capacity. Any services of a financial institution which are unprofitable to the financial institution will be discontinued; the Author doubts any will be discontinued, as all speed financial transaction and lessen accounting necessities. Normal Wage returns for financial capital will result; as Banker joins Depositor in desire for the proper financial return.

The overall pattern of the American Economy can be modified to propel economic performance, without basic alteration of American rules of business procedure. Most of the economic initiatives forwarded in this Work seek to cancel inequities which retard normal market forces. Total Lawyer proceeds in this Nation exceed most budgets of any given State government; all due to liability judgements beyond any economic duress. Feather-bedding in Civil Service—Federal, State, and Local—costs more than Education in this Country; welfare recipients could have their allotments tripled from the savings of reform. The Health industry grows as Cost to American lifestyle at three times any other industry, with industry leaders claiming complete recapitalization for every drug price, while utilizing set labor costs and aged lab facilities to produce a dozen drugs. Health personnel raise labor costs fifty percent for advanced medical training, which rarely takes over three months time, and costs no more than normal college tuition rates. Actual studies indicate Corporate Executives reduce their work load almost as quickly as they increase their salaries; with a business management labor employment for staff growing faster than any other element of business organization.

All elements of the American economic structure moves to cancel the normal market forces All tout as superior. Labor is hired, not to increase economic performance, but to reduce duties of existing personnel. Down-sizing in the Private Sector comes at added cost to production, simply to maximize accounting profits. Financial institution restructure to become Service organizations charging for the process of holding money, rather than as financial aggregation units interested in making a profit for all Participants. The Court system has become a profit-earning industry for lawyers, instead of a Conflict-resolution system. Health has become a growth industry, with a recidivism rate of patient return for the same medical problem at 400% of the rate of forty years ago. Corporation Executives, Lawyers, Doctors, and Civil Servants make up only about three percent of the population, but possess Incomes in total which exceed the total Income of Production employment. It is time for change.

0-595-25098-X

www.ingramcontent.com/pod-product-compliance
Lightning Source LLC
Chambersburg PA
CBHW030816180526
45163CB00003B/1301